2015
CODING
WORKBOOK
for the Physician's Office

2015
CODING
WORKBOOK
for the Physician's Office

Alice Covell, CMA-A (AAMA), RMA, CPC

Gail Smith, MA, RHIA, CCS-P
Technical Editor, 2015 edition

CENGAGE
Learning·

Australia • Brazil • Mexico • Singapore • United Kingdom • United States

CENGAGE
Learning·

2015 Coding Workbook for the Physician's Office
Alice Covell

Gail Smith, Technical Editor, 2015 edition

VP, General Manager, Skills and Planning: Dawn Gerrain

Product Director: Matthew Seeley

Senior Director, Development-Careers and Computing: Marah Bellegarde

Product Manager: Jadin Babin-Kavanaugh

Senior Content Developer: Elisabeth Williams

Editorial Assistant: Mark Turner

Marketing Director: Michele McTighe

Marketing Manager: Erica Glisson

Production Manager: Andrew Crouth

Content Project Management, and Art Direction: Lumina Datamatics, Inc.

For product information and technology assistance, contact us at
Cengage Learning Customer & Sales Support, 1-800-354-9706

For permission to use material from this text or product,
submit all requests online at **www.cengage.com/permissions.**
Further permissions questions can be e-mailed to
permissionrequest@cengage.com

The 2014 versions of CPT, ICD-9-CM, and ICD-10-CM were used in preparation of this product. The HCPCS Level II codes are updated with codes valid in October 2014.

CPT copyright 2015 American Medical Association. All rights reserved. CPT is a registered trademark of the American Medical Association. Applicable FARS/DFARS Restrictions Apply to Government Use. Fee schedules, relative value units, conversion factors and/or related components are not assigned by the AMA, are not part of CPT, and the AMA is not recommending their use. The AMA does not directly or indirectly practice medicine or dispense medical services. The AMA assumes no liability for data contained or not contained herein.

Library of Congress Control Number: 2014959317

Book Only ISBN: 978-1-305-25915-7
Package ISBN: 978-1-305-25913-3

Cengage Learning
20 Channel Center Street
Boston, MA 02210
USA

Cengage Learning is a leading provider of customized learning solutions with office locations around the globe, including Singapore, the United Kingdom, Australia, Mexico, Brazil, and Japan. Locate your local office at **www.cengage.com/global**

Cengage Learning products are represented in Canada by Nelson Education, Ltd.

To learn more about Cengage Learning, visit **www.cengage.com**

Purchase any of our products at your local college store or at our preferred online store **www.cengagebrain.com**

Printed in the United States of America
Print Number: 04   Print Year: 2016

Contents

Preface

Organization of the Text

The *2015 Coding Workbook for the Physician's Office* is organized in the easiest to understand and most logical format currently available in the market for students and instructors alike. The workbook begins with the basics, a brief foundational overview of the importance of coding and the tools necessary to succeed using this text. It is designed to be used in tandem with any main textbook or as supplemental study material.

The workbook begins with coding scenarios for Current Procedural Terminology (CPT), utilizing Evaluation and Management (E/M) codes, and is broken down by body system and then by service performed. The CPT scenarios are followed by HCPCS Level II and CPT and HCPCS Modifiers coding exercises. The bulk of the workbook is comprised of ICD-10-CM and ICD-9-CM coding scenarios. The workbook concludes with case studies, "Putting It All Together," where students can review a case study and provide proper codes based on the practice they've had using the workbook. Answers to the case studies are provided in the back of the workbook.

In the final preparation for students, the workbook offers exam questions for CPT, CPT and HCPCS, and ICD-10-CM. Selected answers from coding exercises are also provided in the back of the book to enhance student comprehension.

New to the *2015 Coding Workbook for the Physician's Office*

As 2015 approaches, so too does the shift to using ICD-10-CM in medical coding. In anticipation of this industry change, the *2015 Coding Workbook for the Physician's Office* includes an updated section entitled "Moving from the old ICD-9-CM to the new ICD-10-CM." This section provides students with an overview of the major changes that medical coding will be facing and challenges students to start coding with ICD-10-CM. Also, "Putting It All Together" includes a column for ICD-10-CM codes in the answers.

In addition to the chapter on ICD-10-CM, a secondary answer column has been provided next to the ICD-10-CM answers for ICD-9-CM. All of the coding scenarios have been updated to be applicable with ICD-10-CM coding guidelines. Students will not only have the benefit of learning to code with the ICD-10-CM system but also supplement their practice and enhance their knowledge with ICD-9-CM codes that may still be used by Worker's Compensation and the auto insurance industry. This significant contribution to the *2015 Coding Workbook for the Physician's Office* embraces the future of coding in the same easy-to-understand and logical format that has been a success since its first publication!

Supplement Package

For the Student

- A 59-day free trial of OptumInsight©'s *EncoderPro.com—Expert* is provided as a bind-in card in the front of the workbook. This software will allow students to look up ICD-9-CM, ICD-10-CM, CPT, and HCPCS Level II codes quickly and accurately across all code sets.
- AAPC continuing education unit (CEU) approval is granted after candidates successfully pass the 30-question exam posted on Cengage Learning's Premium Web site. For more information please see the back page of the workbook.

For the Instructor

- The *Instructor's Manual* is housed online at the Instructor Companion Web site found at www.cengagebrain.com. It serves as an instructional resource and provides answers to coding exercises and test questions for content reinforcement.

EncoderPro.com—Expert 59-Day Free Trial

With the purchase of this textbook you receive free 59-day access to *EncoderPro.com—Expert*, the powerful online medical coding solution from OptumInsight©. With *EncoderPro.com—Expert*, you can simultaneously search across all code sets.

How to Access the Free Trial of *EncoderPro.com—Expert*

Information about how to access your 59-day trial of *EncoderPro.com—Expert* is included on the printed tear-out card bound into this workbook; the card contains a unique user access code and password. Once you log in, scroll down to the bottom of the License Agreement page, and click the "I Accept" link. Then, click the "I Accept" link on the Terms of Use page. Be sure to check with your instructor before beginning your free trial because it will expire 59 days after your initial login.

Features and Benefits of *EncoderPro.com—Expert*

EncoderPro.com—Expert is the essential code lookup software from OptumInsight© for CPT, HCPCS (level II), ICD-9-CM Vol. 1, ICD-9-CM Vol. 3, ICD-10-CM, and ICD-10-PCS code sets. It gives users fast searching capabilities across all code sets. *EncoderPro.com—Expert* can greatly reduce the time it takes to build or review a claim, and it helps improve overall coding accuracy.

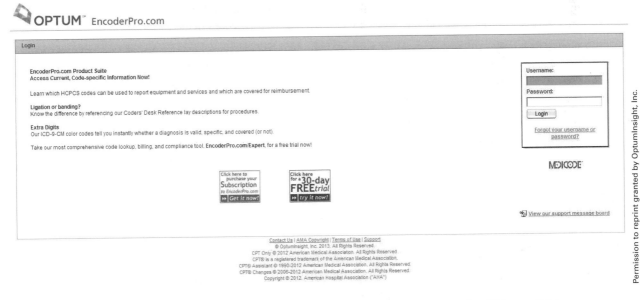

During your free trial period to *EncoderPro.com—Expert*, the following tools will be available to you:

- **Powerful CodeLogic™ search engine.** Search all code sets simultaneously using lay terms, acronyms, abbreviations, and even misspelled words.
- **Lay descriptions for thousands of CPT® codes.** Enhance your understanding of procedures with easy-to-understand descriptions.

- **Color-coded edits.** Understand whether a code carries an age or sex edit, is covered by Medicare, or contains bundled procedures.
- **ICD-10 Mapping Tool.** Crosswalk from ICD-9-CM codes to the appropriate ICD-10 code quickly and easily.
- **Great value.** Get the content from over 20 code and reference books in one powerful solution.

For more information about *EncoderPro.com—Expert* or to become a subscriber beyond the free trial, email us at **esales@cengage.com**.

UNIT I INTRODUCTION TO CODING

Coding and Medical Insurance Policies

Coding can be significant in receiving and keeping payment for medical services. One publication states that coding makes a 25% greater or lesser difference in payment. It is the insurance policy language that defines payable benefits. Beginning coders may ask, "What code do I use to get paid?" A patient who has not received payment may say that the doctor reported the "wrong" code. The answer for both situations is clear. You always use the correct code that supports the documentation.

Doctors often find coding confusing. They may do a new service that does not have a specific code. Do you report it with an existing code number? Sometimes the procedure is not really new, but the doctor uses a new technique or technology. Medicare, the Blues (Blue Cross/Blue Shield), or another payer may notify the doctors to report these services under another code. However, without specific instructions to call the service something different, you should report it under the "unlisted procedure" code. The *Instructions for Use of the CPT Book* emphasize this point by stating, "Do not select a CPT code that merely approximates the service provided. If no such procedure or service exists, then report the service using the appropriate unlisted procedure or service code." The insurer can decide to pay or reject the claim based on the terms of the policy.

Perhaps a new code is now available for a recently developed procedure. Unfortunately, the service may be too new to appear on the insurance policy benefit list and so the payer rejects the claim. The doctor now wonders if you should code it with last year's code. You may decide to make the change after offering explanations to the irate patient who now has a large, unexpected bill. In these no-win situations, it may seem easier to recode and rebill the service. Don't do it. Resist that temptation. The medical record does not support any code but the correct one.

Insurers match the claims with their benefit schedule. Medicare pays for few preventive services. Religious organizations may have policies that do not cover sterilizations or abortions. Payers then send the doctor or policyholder the specified payment or a rejection. If you change the code to make the service payable, it is fraud. Also, a service may not be payable for the diagnosis provided. Suppose the doctor sees a patient for bronchitis and notices that it is time to repeat the electrocardiogram (ECG) as the patient has a family history of heart disease. If the office bills the ECG with the diagnosis of bronchitis, the payer probably will reject the service. Taking an ECG is not a standard procedure for bronchitis and does not support medical necessity. It is correct to report the office visit for bronchitis and the family history of heart disease for the ECG.

Some situations are less clear. No insurer would deny a person the reconstruction of his nose following a serious auto accident, a fall from a horse, or a similar incident. What if the injury occurred 10 years ago? Should the automobile insurer, the owner of the stable, or the patient's own insurance pay the doctor's bill? Is the patient's health insurance primary and expected to pay first before the other insurers? All these health insurance payment problems do not affect the determination of the correct diagnosis and procedure codes.

Medicare and private insurance are separate programs. The Health Insurance Portability and Accountability Act (HIPAA) requires health insurers to adopt the government-approved coding specifications of Medicare and Medicaid. However, Worker's Compensation and the auto insurance industry are exempt from HIPAA and may continue to use the older diagnosis coding system. If you

1

work for a pediatrician, becoming aware of Medicaid rules may be difficult. Pay close attention to payer bulletins and the information on coding distributed at their seminars and workshops. Many private organizations and medical specialty societies offer coding workshops. Try to attend one each year and always end the year with the purchase of new coding references.

Conquering Coding

You may be surprised by how much experience you have with coding. You use it every day. From social security, telephone, and credit card numbers, to thermometers and cable television selectors, numbers that represent words surround us. If you see $1.00, you think "one dollar." Even without a description or explanation, you probably recognize 1-800-555-1212.

Our present diagnosis coding system is ICD-9-CM, the *International Classification of Diseases, Ninth Revision, Clinical Modification*. Disease coding systems began in the late 1800s and identified the causes of death. The ICD system is now used worldwide to record the incidence of disease. Many ICD-9-CM reference books include this history. Take the time to read this fascinating summary of disease recording.

In the near future, we begin to code diagnoses in ICD-10-CM. The 2015 ICD-10-CM is still labeled "draft" with the expectation that ICD-10-CM will replace ICD-9-CM in the next year or so.

The American Medical Association (AMA) developed the procedure or service coding reference, *Current Procedural Terminology (CPT)*. This single volume reference is available from many sources, but the AMA carefully protects the copyright and printing of CPT.

The Health Care Financing Administration (HCFA), now named the Centers for Medicare and Medicaid Services (CMS), the agency responsible for Medicare and Medicaid, recognized that many medical services were not physician services. To report, pay, and monitor ambulance services, medical equipment, and supplies, another set of codes was needed. This system is called the *Healthcare Common Procedure Coding System* or HCPCS (pronounced "hick-picks"). HCPCS has two levels of codes, usually indicated by Roman numerals. The Level I codes are the CPT codes, five digits, or four numbers followed by a letter. Level II codes have a letter followed by four numbers. The Level III codes, or "local" codes, were eliminated with the implementation of the HIPAA standardized code sets in October 2003.

Coding determines the appropriateness of treatment and the medical necessity for a service. Insurers compile statistics on the frequency of a service, sometimes identifying "abused" procedures. They state that many doctors do C-sections for their own convenience rather than patient need, for example. Monitoring the codes billed, Michigan Blue Shield found a physician who performed almost half the endoscopic procedures reported in one year. A Medicaid program discovered a doctor who reported over 400 house calls in one day. The payers, like you, found these data unbelievable, audited the physicians, and recovered the overpayments.

Coding Ground Rules

1. Keep your coding references current. Purchase new books each year.
2. Know the coding rules and apply them properly.
3. Code only what the documentation supports.
4. Match the diagnosis code with the procedure code. They must be "reasonable" and support medical necessity.
5. Review and update all charge tickets, computer files, and encounter forms annually.

UNIT II *CURRENT PROCEDURAL TERMINOLOGY (CPT)*

The American Medical Association (AMA) released the first edition of *Current Procedural Terminology (CPT)* in 1966. It was similar to a coding system called the California Relative Value System (CRVS) developed 10 years earlier by the California Medical Association (CMA). These codes were based on a four-digit system. In 1970, the AMA released the second edition of the CPT code book, adding a fifth digit to the codes to make services more specific. The third edition was printed in 1973 and the fourth edition in 1977. Also, during this time, many insurance companies developed their own coding systems. Some payers used these coding systems internally, and others required the doctor to use these special codes to report services to that insurer.

By 1983, a government study identified over 120 different procedure-coding systems. It was impossible to match services with all these different coding systems, so the government mandated a standard coding system for Medicare and Medicaid. Beginning in 1984, the government required physicians to report all services in HCPCS for all Medicare and Medicaid claims. Also in 1984, the AMA modified the name of CPT and began including the year in the title of the publication.

CPT-1992 changed all the "visit" services, such as office calls, hospital care, and nursing home visits, to Evaluation and Management (E/M) services. In spite of many articles in medical publications, seminars, and newsletters, some physicians still have trouble determining the exact level of care to use for a patient visit. While deciding the correct level of service is the responsibility of the physician, not the medical assistant or biller, we will explore these codes in the worksheets. Medicare required this change as part of their implementation of the Resource Based Relative Value Scale (RBRVS) mandated by Congress to reform the Medicare payment structure.

The present edition of the CPT code book contains over 7,500 different descriptions of services. The AMA protects these codes and descriptions by a copyright. Look at the introductory pages of the current CPT edition where credit is given to the CPT Panel and Advisory Committees responsible for developing these codes. The Table of Contents of the CPT code book shows the organization of the references. Note that the largest section, as you would expect, is the Surgery listing. Appendix B of the CPT code book summarizes the code changes since the last edition. This list identifies the codes you must update in your computer or on office documents. Some CPT code book vendors and AMA have editions with color-coded pages, color keys, and thumb-indexed pages to make it easier to use. Their terminology and illustration sections can provide guidance with unfamiliar terms. It is important to note that there is no separate guide for the use of CPT; the instructions are integrated throughout the code book. The CPT code book's index is not complete, but it can help you search for many codes.

Most successful projects start at the beginning. Look at the CPT code book's Introduction. Many of the higher numbered codes, the E/M services, appear first since most physicians provide these services. A doctor can report a code from any section if that is the service performed. However, the reasonableness of the code must be tested. Would a podiatrist perform neurosurgery? Not likely, but it could appear that way if you transpose digits in the procedure code. The terminology format, with the stem of the procedure before the semicolon, saves space and makes the page easier to read. This code layout is standard in the CPT, HCPCS, and ICD-10-CM references.

Coding guidelines appear in each section of the CPT code book. You must read these carefully to select the correct codes in this workbook. Procedure descriptions may be misleading if you have not read the rules. We will review the "separate procedures" in the surgery section. The "modifiers" do just that; they modify or change a service. They are so important that all modifiers are listed in

Appendix A of the CPT code book. Complete your reading of the CPT's Introduction and review any of the terminology and anatomy pages. Now you are ready to start the worksheets in this workbook.

Evaluation and Management Services

The first three worksheets of *2015 Coding Workbook for the Physician's Office* cover the basic medical visit services provided by almost every health care professional. These are the E/M codes. The service descriptions are complete but confusing. An understanding of terms is critical to accurate interpretation of the services. You must read the CPT definitions of commonly used terms carefully. If you are responsible for billing and have obsolete codes or descriptions on the office encounter or computer forms, change them immediately. You may find an old code or modifier in your computer system. Delete old codes only after making certain you do not need them for statistical use. Contact the vendor of your computer system or software to find the correct procedure for handling obsolete codes and modifiers.

There are three to five levels of many E/M codes. Encounter forms may have a cell labeled "New Patient" and code "99201" listed with the description "Level 1." The guidelines also advise you that the descriptions vary for all Level 1 codes. As you review the instructions, look at the codes used for illustration. Review the instructions on selecting a level of E/M service with the doctors and other professionals so that the documentation in the patient's medical record matches the service level reported.

In the CPT code book, Appendix C provides some clinical examples for each level of service. These are identified by specialty and may help you to select the correct code. Do not read anything into the case study that is not there. If we assumed that the patient was blind, obese, or had another complicating problem, the level of service might change. Base your interpretation on the information provided and nothing else.

Remember our earlier reference to policy benefits deciding whether a code would result in payment? The same rules affect modifiers. Medicare allows the modifier –21, prolonged E/M service, when applied to only the high-level codes. Other payers may not honor or may have special rules for using a specific modifier.

Following the guidelines section, CPT begins with the E/M codes. You will find explanatory information throughout the section. You must read these instructions. Many worksheet items use this additional material. The reformatted visit codes on the next page show the similarities and contrasts for these services. Some criteria are consistent for most codes. New patient services require all three key components: history, examination, and medical decision making. Established patient services need two of the three key components. The wording of the paragraph on counseling and coordination of care is consistent throughout the E/M codes.

The section covering the visit codes may be the most complex in CPT. From here it will become easier. Again, review the guidelines and other instructions carefully as they explain the components of each code.

In 1995, the AMA and HCFA released the documentation standards for E/M services. These described the components of the medical history, and the number of body areas and organ systems that the doctor must examine and document for each level of service. In 1997, HCFA clarified this list by identifying the mandatory elements of the exam. The doctor supports a detailed new patient exam (99203) by documenting 12 to 17 exam items. The complexity of medical decision making is also explained. Be certain there is a copy of these criteria in your office so anyone creating medical

4

records can follow these guidelines. All payers should accept this documentation standard, and the AMA may include it in future editions of CPT.

When the first three E/M services are placed next to each other, it is easier to see the similarities and differences among the codes:

New Patient—99201
(referred to as patient 1)

Office or other outpatient visit for the evaluation and management of a new patient, which requires these three key components:

- A problem-focused history

- A problem-focused examination

- Straightforward medical decision making

Counseling and/or coordination of care with other physicians, other qualified health care professionals, or agencies are provided consistent with the nature of the problem(s) and the patient's or family's needs.

Usually, the presenting problem(s) are self-limited or minor. Typically, 10 minutes face-to-face are spent with the patient or family.

New Patient—99202
(referred to as patient 2)

Office or other outpatient visit for the evaluation and management of a new patient, which requires these three key components:

- An expanded problem-focused history

- An expanded problem-focused examination

- Straightforward medical decision making

Counseling and/or coordination of care with other physicians, other qualified health care professionals, or agencies are provided consistent with the nature of the problem(s) and the patient's or family's needs.

Usually, the presenting problem(s) are of low to moderate severity. Typically, 20 minutes are spent face-to-face with the patient or family.

New Patient—99203
(referred to as patient 3)

Office or other outpatient visit for the evaluation and management of a new patient, which requires these three key components:

- A detailed history

- A detailed examination

- Medical decision making of low complexity

Counseling and/or coordination of care with other physicians, other qualified health care professionals, or agencies are provided consistent with the nature of the problem(s) and the patient's or family's needs.

Usually, the presenting problem(s) are of moderate severity. Typically, 30 minutes are spent face-to-face with the patient or family.

Name _____

Evaluation and Management–I (99201–99239)

2015 CPT Codes

These codes cover office and outpatient visits, hospital daily visits, and medical services for patients in hospital observation units. Most physicians use visit codes, and sometimes they make over 90% of the services performed by a doctor or other qualified health care provider.

Remember, some E/M services may require modifiers.

1. Discussion of medications with the patient admitted yesterday and with the patient's family just before patient left the observation unit   _____

2. Subsequent hospital visit, will discharge patient tomorrow   _____

3. First visit: 2:15 p.m. to 3:20 p.m., multiple complaints: meds for diabetes, arthritis, and hypertension reviewed and changed as patient has rash secondary to present combination; also fulgurated wart on left ring finger   _____

4. Established patient requires brief visit with nurse to verify proper use of inhaler   _____

5. Six-month follow-up visit for patient in aforementioned exercise 3   _____

6. First day in observation unit, patient collapsed at shopping mall and continues to have an irregular heartbeat   _____

7. Patient seen in Emergency Department with severe poison ivy (problem focused history/exam and straightforward medical decision making)   _____

8. Initial office visit for child with chicken pox   _____

9. Eight-year-old girl seen again within 1 month for severe sore throat and fatigue   _____

10. Admission to ICU for 72-year-old male with massive cerebral hemorrhage, respiratory failure, and coma   _____

11. Established patient seen with severe reaction (rash, vomiting) to x-ray study dye, medication prescribed (detailed history/exam with moderate decision making)   _____

12. Comprehensive follow-up counseling visit, emotionally upset over child's behavior and marital problems, 3:15 p.m. to 4:00 p.m.   _____

13. Forty-eight-year-old male admitted to hospital observation unit for chest pain and discharged the same day when all diagnostic studies were within normal limits (comprehensive history/exam and medical decision making of moderate complexity)   _____

14. Spent 20 minutes reviewing improved lab work and discussing results with the patient during subsequent visit to observation unit. Will reduce meds, may discharge from observation tomorrow (problem focused interval history/ examination with moderate decision making)   _____

Name _____

Evaluation and Management–II (99241–99340)

2015 CPT Codes

Consultations occur when one provider requests the *opinion* of another provider. The consultant may perform tests to establish the opinion or may initiate treatment, but the patient remains under the care of the requesting provider. If the consulting physician assumes part or all the care of the patient, it is a referral and not a consultation. A surgeon is usually not a consultant but is expected to take care of the patient's problem. The term *consultation* is sometimes misused, as when the patient *consults* with the doctor. This is reported as an office visit. Consultation codes have two subcategories: office or outpatient and inpatient. Medicare stopped paying consultation codes in 2010, citing misuse. There are also codes for Emergency Services, Critical Care, and Nursing Facility Services, as well as Domiciliary, Rest Home, and Custodial Care Services.

1. Office consult for high school senior with a knee injury that occurred during the homecoming game (detailed history/exam and low decision making) _____

2. Comprehensive admission service for the transfer of a psychotic patient from an acute care hospital to a psychiatric residential treatment center (comprehensive history/exam and moderate complexity decision making) _____

3. Initial hospital detailed consult for male diabetic, had back surgery 3 days ago, has a severe urinary tract infection; procedure scheduled for this afternoon _____

4. One hour in ED with 3-year-old attacked by pit bull, found unconscious with bruises and scrapes, and requires no suturing (detailed history/exam and medical decision making of moderate complexity) _____

5. Annual nursing facility visit _____

6. Brief inpatient consult to rule out abscessed tooth in post-delivery female _____

7. ICU consult for female with cardiac arrest during gallbladder surgery now in a coma _____

8. Office consultation for teenager with severe acne _____

9. Visit to home for the developmentally disabled to see a new patient with recent onset of swelling in hands and feet (expanded problem focused history/exam with decision making of moderate complexity) _____

10. Constant attendance, 1.5 hours critical care in ICU for a 15-year-old male, comatose after diving accident _____

11. Office consult for 58-year-old patient with Alzheimer's and previous stroke now combative and incontinent (comprehensive history/exam with medical decision making of high complexity) _____

12. One-hour discussion with family of an elderly patient being discharged from rehabilitation facility to son's home for aftercare _____

13. Comprehensive ICU history or exam; transfer to surgeon if not improved in 24 hours _____

14. Follow-up skilled nursing facility visit for patient with recent onset of mini-strokes (30 minutes) _____

15. Contacts with family and staff of assisted living facility revising care plan based on recent laboratory studies (July: 22 minutes) _____

16. Established patient with Alzheimer's disease and a urinary tract infection seen at adult care home (expanded problem history/exam and moderate decision making) _____

Name _____

Evaluation and Management–III (99341–99499)

2015 CPT Codes

These codes are used to report home services, prolonged services, physician standby services, case management, team conferences, care plan oversight, preventive medicine, non-face-to-face care, newborn/infant services, and miscellaneous care. They cover special or preventive services that may be excluded under some insurance policies. Be certain the codes you report accurately reflect the services performed so the insurer can appropriately pay or reject the claim. Some services may be payable only for certain diagnoses or in specified locations.

1. Follow-up house call for child recovering from the flu _____

2. Extended follow-up in NICU, unstable 2-month-old infant _____

3. Admission of premature newborn to NICU _____

4. Injured 18-month-old infant transported to Children's Hospital, pediatrician in attendance for 55-minute trip _____

5. One-hour conference at care center with psychologist, nurse, and geriatric assessment staff, pending transfer of patient to long-term care facility; patient not present _____

6. Forty-five minutes of Internet evaluations over the weekend with an established patient not seen in the past month but now threatening suicide _____

7. Initial exam of infant born at home _____

8. NICU visit, 5-day-old infant now weighing 4,200 grams, will transfer to nursery tomorrow _____

9. New patient, annual exam for pilot, age 47 _____

10. Following an EPF visit (99282) in the ED for a 90-year-old patient, the physician spent another hour with the patient's spouse and children contacting long-term care facilities and a geriatric physician to develop a plan of care for the patient _____

11. Standby services (45 minutes) required for cesarean/high-risk delivery _____

12. Counseling on risk factors for sexually active 14-year-old female, 45 minutes _____

13. Preschool exam for 5-year-old child seen since infancy _____

14. Services for the month of June (25 minutes) supervising the hospice team for care of terminally ill cancer patient; patient not seen _____

15. Initial home visit to discuss care options with family of an 88-year-old disabled patient who suffered a stroke one hour ago _____

16. In-office initial management and monitoring of 47-year-old male on Coumadin, nine INR tests and subsequent dosage adjustment, second quarter _____

Name _____

Anesthesia Services (00100–01999)

2015 CPT Codes

Physicians who are not anesthesiologists may report anesthesia services. A doctor may be responsible for the anesthesia when a partner performs a surgical procedure. Some large practices have their own operating room, performing the same procedures in the office that they would do in the hospital outpatient surgicenter. In some cases, an anesthesiologist may not be available. Medical billers should become familiar with these codes and the rules for using them.

Anesthesia use requires some special modifiers, P1 through P6 to indicate the patient's condition and some of the usual CPT modifiers. There are also some 99xxx codes that you bill along with the regular anesthesia service when there are qualifying circumstances. Keep these special rules in mind as you complete the worksheet.

The descriptions do not specify anesthesia, but all answers should come from this section. Watch for procedures that need a modifier or multiple codes.

1. Cervical diagnostic discography injection   _____

2. Abdominal repair, hernia of the diaphragm   _____

3. Vaginal delivery of twins   _____

4. Radiation therapy requiring general anesthesia   _____

5. Total joint replacement, left ankle, for severe arthritis   _____

6. Tenoplasty, left shoulder to elbow   _____

7. Burr holes, critical newborn infant   _____

8. Dual chamber transvenous pacemaker insertion   _____

9. Rhinoplasty, correction of deviated septum   _____

10. Mid-thigh amputation, right leg   _____

11. Lumbar puncture   _____

12. Rectal endoscopy with biopsy   _____

13. Insert umbrella filter, inferior vena cava   _____

14. Pectus excavatum repair, 4-year-old male   _____

15. Arthroscopy, right shoulder   _____

General Surgery Rules

Surgical procedures on the integumentary system begin the extensive surgery section. CPT provides important guidelines for all surgeries. Review them carefully. Then consider the following information as you review the worksheet items.

1. Necessary medical care for diagnostic surgery may be reported separately. Nondiagnostic surgical services include concurrent medical care by the operating surgeon. Other physicians may report medical care that is unrelated to the surgical service. Example: A patient undergoing gallbladder surgery is followed by an internist for chronic emphysema. The internist is paid for the medical care not related to the surgical service. Medicare has comprehensive tables identifying, by procedure code, the days of medical care included in a surgical service. Other insurers may use the same list or have similar restrictions.

2. Surgical services usually include any local anesthesia administered by the operating surgeon.

3. The payment for the surgery includes all related supplies. The doctor may bill for supplies only if they exceed what is usually required for that service. Insurers may refuse to pay for any additional supplies provided by the surgeon. If the surgery is done in the hospital setting, either inpatient or outpatient, payers assume the hospital provided all the necessary supplies.

4. The subsection information contains the special instructions for using a particular range of codes. In some cases, this vital information may appear on the previous page. Always, after you find the code you seek, review the previous page or two for any special rules related to this coding section.

5. A service that is usually part of another service may, on occasion, be reported as the primary surgery. These codes appear throughout CPT and the description ends with "separate procedure." If you perform a service with the "separate procedure" notation, report that service if it is the *only* service performed or is unrelated to the other procedures or services performed. Use the modifier –59, Distinct Procedural Service, to indicate this service is unrelated to the other procedures or services reported. This is a rule many doctors and billers find confusing.

6. Diagnostic endoscopy is included in a surgical endoscopy.

7. Use the unlisted procedure code at the end of each surgery section when there is no code for the service performed. New procedures are reported with these codes until a specific code is assigned. If the service involves a new technique for an established procedure, you would usually report the service with the existing code unless the technique is specified in the description. Note that all unlisted procedure codes end in "9" and many end in "99." Remember, whenever you report these unlisted services, you will need to make the operative notes available or provide a complete description of the service.

8. The special report is similar to the unlisted procedure. Again, you must explain the service completely. Documentation must be sent with the claim. These claims may not be accepted electronically as they require attachments. Some payers have a fax line to receive the required documentation for electronic claims.

9. Some of the CPT surgery modifiers may be listed in the guidelines of each surgery section. All CPT modifiers appear in CPT Appendix A.

10. Some complications may be reported in addition to the surgery using the modifier –22 and a detailed explanation. Medicare will usually reject any medical care billed by the surgeon during the specified postoperative period. To get paid, the surgeon must establish that the medical care rendered is not part of the usual postoperative care for the previous surgery.

11. Modifiers –54, –55, and –56 cover situations where the surgeon does not provide all the medical care related to the surgery. Physicians other than the surgeon may provide and be paid for medical care related to the surgery if the surgeon indicates his service does not include the preoperative or postoperative medical care.

12. Sometimes the doctor performs multiple procedures. If the surgery is a bilateral carpal tunnel release, you may be instructed by the payer to report the code and the modifier –50 or to report two identical lines, one with modifier –RT and the other with modifier –LT. Suppose the patient has gallbladder surgery and the doctor also removes nevi from the left neck and left thigh, and a basal cell CA of the scalp. You would report the major procedure on the first line, the basal cell CA on the second line, and the nevi on subsequent lines in the order of diminishing significance. The modifier –51 would be used on all but the first service line. Exception: See the following point 14. Payers develop policies for use of modifier –51. Also, each service line must show the appropriate diagnosis code reference number.

13. Therapeutic surgery includes all related medical care. The modifier –24 is used when the surgeon performs a separate, postoperative medical service unrelated to the surgical procedure. Example: A patient had a surgery last week but now visits the surgeon's office for an acute asthma attack. If the asthma is unrelated to the surgery, the office visit may be billed as a separate service with modifier –24.

14. Some multiple surgical procedures must be reported without modifier –51. These are the "add-on" codes, identified in CPT Appendix D. Because these codes are added on to the reporting of another code, they can never be used alone.

15. CPT Appendix E lists the CPT codes that are not "add-on" codes but do not require the modifier –51. Codes such as 20975 (electrical stimulation to aid bone healing, invasive, operative) or 31500 (intubation, endotracheal, emergency procedure) are billable but may be related to another reported service. Watch this Appendix closely if you perform these services as this list is updated yearly. Medicare rejects these codes as incorrectly reported if modifier –51 is attached.

Modifiers increase in importance every year. Each new edition of CPT and HCPCS bring changes in the familiar ones and new modifiers. Be certain you review the modifier sections when you look for changes in procedure codes.

Medicare and most other payers reject "unbundling," the reporting of multiple services when one code includes all procedures. When physicians code from a list, they may miss a code that contains multiple services. Encounter forms or coding sheets may state:

51840	Marshall-Marchetti
58150	Abdominal Hysterectomy
58700	Salpingectomy(ies)
58940	Oophorectomy(ies)

Turn to code 58150. The description includes codes 58700 and 58940. Suppose the patient with the abdominal hysterectomy also had a Marshall-Marchetti type procedure. The correct code, 58152, contains all the aforementioned procedures. The CMS rebundling list is called the "National Correct Coding Initiative" or NCCI and is revised quarterly. Many insurance carriers implement these policies as soon as CMS releases them.

Caution: The CPT worksheets may require multiple procedure codes, a modifier, or the reporting of quantity. Any time the CPT code says "each," you need to report a quantity, even if it is only one. As you complete the worksheets, pronounce the terms. You can increase your vocabulary as you expand your coding skills.

Integumentary System

These codes include procedures on the skin, subcutaneous and accessory structures, nail, and breast. They cover the removal of lesions, suturing, plastic repairs, burn treatment, and other surgeries. Read the embedded instructions immediately under the headings "Removal of Skin Tags" and "Shaving of Epidermal or Dermal Lesions." Would we report suturing with the shaving of a dermal lesion? No, because the notation states that "the wound does not require suture closure."

Look at CPT's Rule 2 for Repair (Closure) when repairing multiple lacerations. Add together the length of all wounds in the same classification and report the total as a single item. This rule does not apply to excising multiple lesions, as each is reported individually. Documentation of inches or millimeters must be translated to centimeters, the standard measurement for reporting lesions.

Before beginning the worksheets, look at the codes and read the text of the entire integumentary section. You may wish to have a medical dictionary and anatomy reference handy. Benign lesions are listed before malignant; suturing is simple, intermediate, and complex; and the miscellaneous categories list services that do not fit into other sections. The integumentary system ends with procedures on the breast.

Note: Watch for worksheet items requiring a modifier, quantity, or multiple codes.

Name _____

Integumentary System (10021–19499)

2015 CPT Codes

1. Hair transplant, 21 punch grafts _____

2. Removal of 16 skin tags from neck and chest _____

3. Removal of Norplant contraceptive capsules _____

4. Simple blepharoplasty, right upper lid _____

5. Reclosure, surgical dehiscence _____

6. Debridement of skin and subcutaneous tissue, left forearm (5 sq. cm.) _____

7. Permanent removal distal half, left great toenail _____

8. Full thickness free skin graft 2 × 5 cm., left cheek _____

9. Simple shoulder biopsy of a single skin lesion _____

10. Adjacent tissue transfer, back, 8 sq. cm. _____

11. Laser destruction, benign 2 cm. facial lesion _____

12. Excision/Z-plasty repair, 11 sq. cm. forehead lesion _____

13. Aspiration, breast cyst, right _____

14. Burn site preparation of back, 4%, 9-year-old female _____

15. Wound suture, 3/4" right hand, 1/2" left foot _____

16. Breast reduction, left _____

17. Excision, simple repair, right axillary hidradenitis _____

18. Xenograft, left thigh, 4 × 8 cm. _____

19. Excise malignant 1/2" lesion, neck _____

20. I&D (incision and drainage) hematoma, left hand _____

21. Major debridement of partial thickness burns, both legs _____

22. Mohs micrographic surgery for basal cell carcinoma of the nose. Two-stage procedure: 1st stage four tissue blocks and 2nd stage five tissue blocks _____

23. Debridement and removal of gravel and glass from skin and subcutaneous tissue of open fracture wound _____

24. Split autograft, back (2% body area), 2-year-old male _____

25. Lipectomy, right buttock _____

Musculoskeletal System

Three worksheets on the musculoskeletal system cover the largest unit in the surgery section. They describe procedures on the supporting structures of the body such as bone, muscle, and tendon. The first worksheet includes trauma, excision or removal, replantation, grafting, the head, neck and thorax, spine, abdomen, and shoulder. The second worksheet has procedures on the arm, hand and fingers, and pelvis and hip joint. The third involves services on the femur, knee, leg, ankle, and foot and concludes with casting, strapping, and arthroscopy.

The many rules and definitions appearing within the section give specific instructions on coding. Note that the service includes the first cast or traction device. This information is repeated at the start of the casting section. There are also modifiers to identify the service as right or left, and ones that identify specific digits.

Some doctors use the terms "closed" and "open" to describe both the fracture and the treatment. If this is happening in your office, talk to the provider and get the treatment clarified before billing the service.

The musculoskeletal system is arranged by body site, from the top down, from the center out. After the general procedures, it is organized:

1. Head
2. Neck and thorax
3. Back and flank
4. Spine
5. Abdomen
6. Shoulder
7. Humerus and elbow
8. Forearm and wrist
9. Hand and fingers
10. Pelvis and hip joint
11. Femur and knee joint
12. Leg and ankle joint
13. Foot and toes
14. Casts and strapping
15. Endoscopy or arthroscopy

Most body site sections follow this organization:

1. Incision
2. Excision
3. Introduction or removal
4. Repair, revision, reconstruction
5. Fracture or dislocation
6. Arthrodesis
7. Amputation
8. Miscellaneous

Note how many worksheet items in the musculoskeletal section contain the diagnosis. Always exercise caution when selecting the ICD-9-CM diagnosis for the terms included in the procedure description. Watch for items that need multiple procedure codes; right, left, finger, and toe modifiers; or quantity specified.

Name _____

Musculoskeletal System–I (20005–23929)

2015 CPT Codes

1. Percutaneous needle biopsy, right deltoid muscle _____

2. Partial acromionectomy, left shoulder _____

3. Wick monitoring with compression measurements, muscle compartment syndrome, right leg _____

4. Four segment kyphectomy _____

5. Injection service for left TMJ arthrogram _____

6. LeFort II reconstruction, two autografts _____

7. Removal of total right shoulder prosthesis for replacement _____

8. Closed reduction of fractured mandible with dental fixation _____

9. Maxillectomy, extra oral osteotomy, for cyst _____

10. Radical sternal resection with major bone graft for osteomyelitis (two codes) _____

11. Remove external wire fixation under anesthesia _____

12. Posterior open treatment of two thoracic vertebrae _____

13. Right shoulder arthrodesis, no graft _____

14. Care of simple closed nasal fracture, no manipulation or stabilization _____

15. Right total shoulder replacement _____

16. Reattachment of completely severed right thumb tip _____

17. Anterior osteotomy, discectomy, two thoracic vertebrae (two codes) _____

18. Medrol injection, right hip _____

19. Exploratory arthrotomy, left A-C joint _____

20 Open treatment blowout fracture, transantral, right orbit _____

21. Microvascular anastomosis, osteocutaneous flap, left great toe _____

22. Custom prosthesis preparation, left ear _____

23. Exploration of chest, multiple gunshot wounds _____

24. I&D deep soft tissue, osteomyelitic abscess, left buttock _____

25. Exploration of fusion, lumbar spine _____

Name _____

Musculoskeletal System–II (23930–27299)

2015 CPT Codes

1. Open repair of left Dupuytren's contracture   _____

2. Hypothenar opponensplasty, right   _____

3. Open Bennett fracture with internal fixation, left   _____

4. Secondary flexor repair and graft, right no man's land   _____

5. Synovial biopsy of right elbow by arthrotomy   _____

6. Manipulation lunate dislocation, closed   _____

7. Darrach procedure, left   _____

8. Decompression fasciotomy, extensor, left wrist   _____

9. ORIF (open reduction internal fixation) right olecranon   _____

10. Right Z-plasty fasciectomy with release of 3rd and 4th IP joints
    (multiple codes)   _____

11. Repair nonunion of left radius without graft   _____

12. Closed manipulation of traumatic left hip dislocation, no anesthesia   _____

13. Flap repair, syndactyly, right 4th web space   _____

14. Removal of recurrent ganglion, left wrist   _____

15. Transmetacarpal reamputation, left first finger   _____

16. Subfascial soft tissue biopsy, right forearm   _____

17. Percutaneous pinning, left epicondylar fracture   _____

18. Closed manipulation MP dislocation left 4th finger, with anesthesia   _____

19. Saucerization distal phalanx, left ring finger   _____

20. Total hip arthroplasty, right. Replaced the femoral and acetabular components.   _____

21. Remove implant, revise arthroplasty, left wrist joint   _____

22. Opposition fusion and graft, left thumb   _____

23. Microvascular toe-to-hand transfer 2nd and 3rd toe to previous bone graft,
    left hand   _____

24. Right femur, epiphyseal arrest by stapling   _____

25. Reinsert ruptured left distal triceps tendon with graft   _____

Name _____

Musculoskeletal System–III (27301–29999)

2015 CPT Codes

1. Right shoulder arthroscopy with lysis of adhesions _____

2. Phalangectomy, left 3rd toe _____

3. Exploration with synovial biopsy by arthrotomy, left knee _____

4. Release of left tarsal tunnel _____

5. Left knee arthroscopy, sewing needle removed _____

6. Fracture right medial malleolus, closed treatment, no manipulation _____

7. Surgical correction with fixation, left patellar fracture _____

8. Gastrocnemius neurectomy, left _____

9. Heyman midtarsal capsulotomy, right _____

10. Lengthening multiple bilateral hamstring tendons _____

11. I&D hematoma, left ankle _____

12. Arthroscopy with left medial meniscus repair _____

13. Fracture femoral shaft, open with screws, left _____

14. Right Joplin bunion repair _____

15. Repair of severed collateral ligament, right ankle _____

16. Knock-knee osteotomy, left, before closure _____

17. Lengthening, left Achilles tendon _____

18. Plantar fasciotomy, left, by arthroscopy _____

19. Goldwaite procedure for dislocating patella, right _____

20. Manipulation right trimalleolar fracture _____

21. Guillotine amputation, left tibia/fibula _____

22. Application of right long arm splint _____

23. Left sesamoid fracture, closed treatment _____

24. Revision right long leg cast, walker heel applied _____

25. Right great toe IP joint arthrodesis _____

Respiratory System

From nosebleed and tonsillectomy to removal of a lung, this section covers procedures associated with the nose, sinuses, larynx, trachea, bronchi, lungs, and pleura.

In this system, we are introduced to endoscopy. Note that when a surgical or therapeutic endoscopy is performed, the appropriate sinusotomy, diagnostic endoscopy, and inspecting all sinuses code is included. This is another example of correct coding or bundling of services.

Name _____

Respiratory System (30000–32999)

2015 CPT Codes

1. Partial removal, left inferior turbinate   _____

2. Split cricoid laryngoplasty   _____

3. Endoscopy with A&P ethmoidectomy   _____

4. Closure nasoseptal perforations from cocaine use   _____

5. Bronchoscopy with laser destruction of lesions   _____

6. Open tube thoracostomy for empyema   _____

7. External arytenoidopexy   _____

8. Revision of tracheostoma   _____

9. Video-assisted thoracic surgery [VATS] performed for a biopsy of pericardial sac _____

10. Intranasal antrotomy, right   _____

11. Plastic repair closure of tracheostomy   _____

12. Intrathoracic tracheoplasty   _____

13. Tracheobronchoscopy through tracheostomy   _____

14. Direct laryngoscopy with biopsy, via microscope   _____

15. Surgical nasal endoscopy, polypectomy   _____

16. Secondary major rhinoplasty   _____

17. Removal of toy from nose, 2-year-old male, in office   _____

18. Pneumonolysis with packing   _____

19. Radical neck, partial laryngectomy for CA   _____

20. Unilateral sinusotomy, three sinuses, right   _____

21. Polypectomy, office surgery   _____

22. Empyemectomy   _____

23. Surgical endoscopy, repair sphenoid CSF leak   _____

24. Left thoracoscopy, with wedge resection   _____

25. Needle aspiration, left lung   _____

Cardiovascular System

This section lists the surgical procedures on the vascular and cardiac systems: the heart, veins, and arteries. The instructional introductory paragraphs refer to first, second, and third-order vessels and vascular families and the injection procedures for arteriography.

The Society of Interventional Radiology (SIR) distributes an excellent reference explaining the family trees of the vascular system. This book is available on their Web site.

Excellent cardiovascular coding references are available from the American College of Cardiology or the CPT Reference Guide for Cardiovascular Coding, updated annually and available from the AMA.

Because surgery on the cardiovascular system usually represents major surgery, there are few codes identified as "separate procedure." Operations on the arteries and veins include the intraoperative angiogram. Aortic procedures include the sympathectomy, if performed. Diagnostic cardiac catheterization is in the Medicine section.

Review the extensive explanation of pacemaker and cardioverter-defibrillator services. Coronary bypass grafting, both venous and arterial, is complex and requires careful reading.

Caution: Watch out for worksheet item 3. Move slowly and carefully through this CPT section.

Name _____

Cardiovascular System (33010–37799)

2015 CPT Codes

1. Short saphenous vein stripping, left leg   _____

2. Vein graft repair, left brachial artery   _____

3. Coronary bypass grafts, one venous and two arterial   _____

4. Direct repair of vertebral artery aneurysm   _____

5. Relocation of pacemaker pocket   _____

6. Percutaneous transcatheter removal of broken arterial catheter fragment   _____

7. Open atrial septostomy with bypass   _____

8. Insertion of permanent pacemaker with electrodes inserted in the right atrium
   and ventricle   _____

9. Needle placement, left jugular vein   _____

10. Removal of implanted arterial infusion pump   _____

11. Pulmonary artery embolectomy without bypass   _____

12. Mitral valvotomy with bypass   _____

13. Cardiectomy with heart transplant   _____

14. Creation of AV shunt; direct anastomosis of radial artery and
    cephalic vein   _____

15. Diagnostic arterial puncture   _____

16. Cut down venipuncture, newborn   _____

17. Splenorenal bypass, synthetic graft   _____

18. Percutaneous transluminal fem-pop atherectomy, left   _____

19. Direct repair of ruptured splenic artery aneurysm   _____

20. Mitral valve ring annuloplasty with CP bypass   _____

21. Repeat pericardiocentesis   _____

22. Repair lacerated aorta with cardiopulmonary bypass   _____

23. Resection with commissurotomy for infundibular stenosis   _____

24. Ligation/repair patent ductus arteriosus, 19-year-old female   _____

25. Patch closure of ventricular septal defect   _____

Hemic and Lymphatic Systems—Mediastinum and Diaphragm

These combined, small sections include procedures on the spleen, bone marrow, stem cell services or procedures, lymph nodes and channels, mediastinum, and diaphragm.

Compared to the cardiovascular section, this one is easy.

Note how many services are designated as "separate procedure." These services may be performed at the same time and setting of other major procedures and are not reported separately.

Name _____

Hemic and Lymphatic Systems—Mediastinum and Diaphragm (38100–39599)

2015 CPT Codes

1.   Superficial needle biopsy of inguinal lymph node   _____

2.   Complete right axillary lymphadenectomy   _____

3.   Repair acute traumatic hernia of diaphragm   _____

4.   Insertion of thoracic duct cannula   _____

5.   Drainage of single lymph node abscess, left axilla   _____

6.   Laparoscopic splenectomy   _____

7.   Open excision of deep axillary node, right   _____

8.   Radical retroperitoneal lymphadenectomy   _____

9.   Lymphangiotomy   _____

10. Mediastinoscopy with biopsy   _____

11. Partial splenectomy for traumatic injury   _____

12. Superficial inguinofemoral lymphadenectomy   _____

13. Retroperitoneal staging lymphadenectomy   _____

14. Correct newborn diaphragmatic hernia, insert chest tube   _____

15. Needle bone marrow biopsy   _____

16. Suprahyoid lymphadenectomy, right   _____

17. Eventration of paralytic diaphragm   _____

18. Deep jugular node dissection × 3   _____

19. Allogenic bone marrow transplant   _____

20. Injection for lymphangiography, bilateral   _____

21. Resection of benign neoplasm from mediastinum   _____

22. Staging, partial pelvic lymphadenectomy   _____

23. Excise left axillary hygroma, deep neurovascular dissection   _____

24. Repair ruptured spleen   _____

25. Total pelvic lymphadenectomy by laparoscope   _____

Current Procedural Terminology ©2014 American Medical Association. All Rights Reserved.

Digestive System

This system covers procedures on the lips, mouth, palate, salivary glands, pharynx, adenoids, tonsils, esophagus, stomach, intestines, appendix, rectum and anus, liver, biliary tract, pancreas, abdomen, peritoneum, and omentum as well as bariatric surgery and hernia repair.

This diverse section contains endoscopic procedures and refers to the related radiographic guidance, supervision, and interpretation services. Remember that surgical endoscopy includes diagnostic endoscopy.

Watch for multiple codes and the items that require a modifier.

Name _____

Digestive System (40490–49999)

2015 CPT Codes

1. I&D peritonsillar abscess   _____

2. Flexible esophagoscopy with removal of a piece of hard candy   _____

3. Open Roux-en-Y bypass for obesity   _____

4. Fredet-Ramstedt pyloromyotomy   _____

5. Hemicolectomy, combination of abdominal and transanal approach _____

6. Commando glossectomy   _____

7. Initial inguinal hernia repair with mesh, 32-year-old male   _____

8. Transsacral proctectomy   _____

9. Rubber band ligature hemorrhoidectomy   _____

10. ERCP with placement of stent in pancreatic duct   _____

11. Stomal colonoscopy for control of hemorrhage   _____

12. Esophagogastroduodenoscopy, balloon dilation of obstructed outlet _____

13. Laparoscopic adjustment gastric lap band   _____

14. Second stage, primary bilateral cleft lip repair   _____

15. Colonoscopy with laser destruction of a polyp   _____

16. Subsequent peritoneal lavage with imaging   _____

17. Rectal stricture dilation under general anesthesia   _____

18. Cholecystectomy with cholangiography   _____

19. Thoracic closure of esophagostomy   _____

20. Flexible sigmoidoscopy with biopsy   _____

21. Partial left lobe hepatectomy   _____

22. Salivary gland biopsy by incision   _____

23. Hepaticoenterostomy by U-tube   _____

24. Removal of dental implant, left mandible   _____

25. Plastic repair of pharynx   _____

Urinary System

This section includes the procedures on the kidneys, ureters, bladder, prostate, and urethra and also transplant services including the harvesting of the kidney. Urinary endoscopy and other procedures identify special bundling instructions.

Caution: Read the worksheet items carefully. "Urethra" and "ureter" can look similar in some forms of the words. Note the different codes for male and female.

One worksheet item has two possible codes. What else do you need to know to find the exact code?

Name _____

Urinary System (50010–53899)

2015 CPT Codes

1. Cystourethroscopy for initial insertion of permanent adjustable transprostatic implant (UroLift® system)   _____

2. Transurethral resection of prostate, complete   _____

3. Closure of traumatic kidney wound   _____

4. Infant meatotomy   _____

5. Cystourethroscopy, fulguration of 1.9 cm. tumor   _____

6. Complete cystectomy, bilateral lymphadenectomy   _____

7. Bowel anastomosis with ureterocolon conduit, right   _____

8. Repair of ureterovisceral fistula   _____

9. Needleless EMG study of anal sphincter   _____

10. Subsequent dilation urethra, 21-year-old female, no anesthesia   _____

11. Cystourethroscopy, steroid treatment of stricture   _____

12. Suprapubic catheter bladder aspiration   _____

13. Exploratory nephrotomy   _____

14. Partial excision of left kidney   _____

15. Excision of Cowper's gland   _____

16. Sling procedure for incontinence, 43-year-old male   _____

17. Ureterolithotomy, stone in upper third   _____

18. Plastic repair of ureter stricture   _____

19. Litholapaxy, 2.7 cm. calculus   _____

20. Marshall-Marchetti-Kranz procedure   _____

21. Cystometrogram   _____

22. Injection procedure for chain urethrocystography   _____

23. Percutaneous placement of ureteral stent   _____

24. Bilateral pyeloplasty for horseshoe kidney   _____

25. Laser vaporization of prostate with TURP   _____

Male Genital System, Including Intersex Surgery

These codes identify procedures on the penis, testes, epididymis, tunica vaginalis, scrotum, vas deferens, spermatic cord, seminal vesicles, and prostate.

Because there are only two codes, intersex surgery is included in this section.

Watch for the worksheet item that has two possible answers.

Name _____

Male Genital System, Including Intersex Surgery (54000–55899)

2015 CPT Codes

1.   Newborn clamp circumcision _____

2.   Traumatic partial amputation of penis _____

3.   Punch biopsy of prostate _____

4.   Bilateral hydrocelectomy _____

5.   Radical retropubic prostatectomy _____

6.   Urethroplasty, 3rd stage Cecil repair _____

7.   Electroejaculation _____

8.   Implantation of prosthetic testicle, left _____

9.   Bilateral vasectomy _____

10. Chemical destruction of penile condyloma _____

11. Exploration of scrotum _____

12. Complex scrotoplasty _____

13. Insertion of radioactive pellet in prostate _____

14. One stage repair, perineal hypospadias with tube _____

15. Radical orchiectomy, abdominal exploration _____

16. Insertion of inflatable penile prosthesis _____

17. Abdominal vesiculectomy, right _____

18. Varicocelectomy with hernia repair _____

19. Abdominal exploration for undescended testes, bilateral _____

20. Plethysmography of penis _____

21. Biopsy and exploration of epididymis _____

22. Testicular biopsy via needle _____

23. Bilateral venous shunt for priapism _____

24. Complex incision into the prostate gland for drainage of abscess _____

25. Sex change surgery, male to female _____

Female Genital System and Maternity

This section defines reproductive system procedures; procedures on the vulva, perineum and introitus, vagina, cervix and corpus uteri, oviducts, and ovaries; and in vitro fertilization. Also included are the maternity services related to delivery, antepartum, and postpartum care.

There are several options for endoscopy in this section. You may need to read the procedure notes before coding the vulvar surgery as simple, radical, partial, or complete.

Note the services included in the prenatal or antepartum care. The instructions state: "other visits or services within this time period should be coded separately." This means that if you see a maternity patient for the flu or a burn, and you code it as unrelated to the pregnancy, you may bill it as an additional service. Would you bill inpatient medical care for the time your patient is hospitalized for delivery? No, not for the usual care associated with delivery, but you could report additional care for other complications. Also, another physician following the patient for an unrelated difficulty, such as a cardiac problem, would bill for regular medical care as it is not related to the delivery.

Examine the instructions on partial prenatal care. Note that *abortion*, not *miscarriage*, is the correct term for an uncompleted pregnancy. Abortions may be spontaneous, incomplete, missed, septic, or induced.

Some worksheet items may require multiple codes or quantity indicators.

Female Genital System and Maternity (55920–59899)

2015 CPT Codes

1. Removal of three small leiomyomata with total weight of 200 grams by laparoscopy _____

2. Repair of rectovaginal fistula with colostomy, abdominal approach _____

3. Intrauterine embryo transfer _____

4. Diagnostic amniocentesis _____

5. Cervical colposcopy, LEEP biopsy, small electrode _____

6. Tubal occlusion with ring _____

7. Surgical treatment of second trimester missed abortion _____

8. Cystocele/urethrocele repair _____

9. Chorionic villus sampling by needle _____

10. Laparoscopic excision of pelvic lesions _____

11. Injection of dye for hysterosalpingogram _____

12. Salpingectomy for ectopic pregnancy, by laparoscopy _____

13. Vaginal delivery with external cephalic version _____

14. Vaginal excision, three uterine fibroids, 240 grams _____

15. Cervical stump excision with repair of pelvic floor using an abdominal approach _____

16. Vaginal hysterectomy, partial vaginectomy, enterocele repair _____

17. Vaginal trachelorrhaphy _____

18. Laser destruction of extensive vaginal lesions _____

19. Complete pelvic exenteration _____

20. Bilateral excision of ovarian cysts _____

21. C-section delivery with postpartum care _____

22. Tubal ligation, one day after delivery _____

23. Fascial sling for stress incontinence _____

24. Biopsy perineum, two lesions _____

25. Hysteroscopy, lysis of adhesions _____

Endocrine and Nervous Systems

Procedures on the thyroid, parathyroid, thymus, and adrenal glands; pancreas; carotid body; skull, meninges, and brain; spine and spinal cord; extracranial and peripheral nerves; and autonomic nervous system; as well as destruction by neurolytic agent, neuroplasty, and neurorrhaphy are included in this worksheet.

The nervous system surgery is categorized by approach, definitive surgery, and reconstruction services that may be performed by more than one surgeon. You may want to refer to an anatomy text for clarification of the complex neurosurgical procedures.

Caution: Worksheet items 6 and 23: Don't forget modifiers and quantity where needed.

Endocrine and Nervous Systems (60000–64999)

2015 CPT Codes

1. Subtotal thyroidectomy with radical neck dissection   _____

2. Transcranial orbital exploration, removal of bullet   _____

3. Intra-abdominal avulsion, vagus nerve   _____

4. Laminectomy and excision of intradural sacral lesion   _____

5. Single nerve graft, left arm, 4.5 cm.   _____

6. Injection procedure, lumbar discogram (L4–L5)   _____

7. Decompressive resection, single cervical vertebral body (anterior approach)   _____

8. Remove and replace CSF shunt system   _____

9. Percutaneous stereotactic chemical lesion, trigeminal   _____

10. Excision of thyroid adenoma   _____

11. Paracervical nerve block for delivery   _____

12. Repeat subdural tap through suture, newborn   _____

13. Excision with graft of infected intradural bone   _____

14. Total removal of implanted spinal neurostimulator receiver   _____

15. Bone flap craniotomy for cerebellopontine tumor   _____

16. Suture thenar motor nerve, right hand   _____

17. Exploratory burr hole, supratentorial, bilateral   _____

18. Repair complex dural intracranial AV malformation   _____

19. Cervical hemilaminectomy/re-exploration and decompression   _____

20. Brain stem biopsy, transoral/split mandible approach   _____

21. Excision of carotid body tumor and artery   _____

22. Craniectomy for posterior fossa tumor   _____

23. Cable nerve grafts, 3 cm. right arm and 4.5 cm. left leg   _____

24. LeFort osteotomy with fixation, anterior fossa   _____

25. Cranioplasty for 6.5 cm. skull defect   _____

Eye and Ocular Adnexa

This section lists procedures on the eyeballs, cornea, iris, ciliary body, lens, vitreous, retina, eye muscles, bony orbit, eyelids, conjunctiva, and lacrimal system.

Note the distinction between ocular and orbital implants. There are many laser procedures for the eye. Removal of a cataract may include other services. The surgeon may do the lens implant as a single stage procedure at the time the cataract is removed, or later.

Since there are two eyes and two ears, the -RT and -LT modifiers are especially important in the next two sections.

Watch for add-on or multiple codes and modifiers.

Eye and Ocular Adnexa (65091–68899)

2015 CPT Codes

1. Probe/irrigate left nasolacrimal duct under general anesthesia _____

2. One laser treatment session, three small retinal breaks, left _____

3. Exploration left orbit, remove embedded nailhead _____

4. Excise 0.75 cm. conjunctival lesion, left eye _____

5. Reinsert ocular implant with conjunctival graft, right _____

6. Revise operative site, right anterior segment _____

7. Removal of posterior foreign body with magnet, OS _____

8. Left tarsal wedge excision for ectropion _____

9. Peripheral iridectomy for glaucoma, left _____

10. Correction of right surgical astigmatism by wedge _____

11. External levator repair, right blepharoptosis _____

12. Enucleation, insertion of muscle stabilized implant, left _____

13. Repeat scleral buckling, old retinal detachment, left _____

14. Excise lower lid chalazions, three left, one right _____

15. Right corneal laceration repair with tissue glue _____

16. Laser treatment of left vitreous strands _____

17. Removal of right dacryolith _____

18. Laser trabeculoplasty, right _____

19. Discission of left secondary cataract by incision _____

20. Total reconstruction, right upper lid _____

21. Extracapsular phacoemulsification with lens implant, left _____

22. Posterior fixation for strabismus, resect two horizontal muscles, OD _____

23. Single plug closure, right lacrimal punctum _____

24. Bilateral antibiotic injection, anterior chamber _____

25. Initial superior oblique strabismus surgery, left _____

Auditory System

This section includes procedures on the external, middle, and inner ear, and the temporal bone. After the eye, coding the ear services seems easy.

Caution: One worksheet item needs an add-on code; most need modifiers.

Auditory System (69000–69990)

2015 CPT Codes

1. Replace left temporal bone conduction device _____

2. Bilateral otoplasty for severely protruding ears _____

3. Total facial nerve suture and graft with operating microscope _____

4. Repeat right mastoidectomy, now radical _____

5. Excision of right external ear cyst _____

6. Neurectomy, right tympanic membrane _____

7. Postauricular middle ear exploration, left _____

8. Simple mastoidectomy, right _____

9. Semicircular canal fenestration, left _____

10. Stapedotomy, repair of right ossicular chain _____

11. Catheterize/inflate left eustachian tube, transnasal _____

12. Right oval window fistula repair _____

13. Facial nerve repair, intratemporal (medial to geniculate ganglion) left _____

14. Left tube tympanostomy with Novocaine _____

15. Subtotal amputation, right external ear _____

16. Cochlear implant, right _____

17. Excision polyp from external left ear _____

18. Remove foreign body from left external ear under general anesthesia _____

19. I&D of abscess, left external meatus _____

20. Myringoplasty, right _____

21. Left mastoidectomy with labyrinthectomy _____

22. Excision of benign neoplasm, left temporal bone _____

23. Mastoidectomy/tympanoplasty with reconstruction, right ossicular chain _____

24. Excision left extratemporal glomus tumor _____

25. Routine cleaning of right mastoid cavity _____

Radiology

The first worksheet of radiographic procedures covers the section on diagnostic radiology and imaging. It includes flat films of the head and neck, chest, spine, pelvis, and upper and lower extremities. These studies are the most common radiologic procedures performed in the physician's office if the practice has the appropriate equipment.

The second worksheet includes studies of the abdomen, gastrointestinal and urinary tracts, and gynecological and obstetrical services. It also includes diagnostic imaging of the heart, aorta and arteries, and veins and lymphatics. It concludes with transcatheter procedures, transluminal atherectomy, and other therapeutic procedures.

The third worksheet covers three sections. The first section, diagnostic ultrasound or *echo*, includes procedures for diagnosis and guidance. The second section, radiation oncology, provides codes for clinical treatment planning, delivery and management, hyperthermia, and brachytherapy. The last section, diagnostic nuclear medicine, has codes for the endocrine, lymphatic, gastrointestinal, musculoskeletal, cardiovascular, respiratory, nervous, and genitourinary systems, and therapeutic nuclear studies.

Radiology services, with 70000 to 79999 codes, is one of the nonsurgical sections in CPT. This section has special instructions, unlisted procedure codes, and modifiers. The "supervision and interpretation" (S&I) services correspond to many of the injection procedures in previous surgical sections. Many of the "S&I" codes are followed by a reference to the surgical part of the diagnostic service. The Interventional Radiology Coding Users' Guide is very helpful in explaining these services.

Many specialists perform S&I studies, not just radiologists. Note that a written report, signed by the doctor interpreting the study, is part of the service and may not be billed separately. Nuclear medicine, once limited to the hospital setting, is now part of some medical practices.

Remember that the service at the doctor's office is the global or complete service, both the professional and technical components. The same study performed at the hospital must be reported as the "professional component," as the doctor does not own the equipment. The facility reports the "technical component" to be paid for the equipment, staff, supplies, lights, and other expenses associated with the service. With few exceptions, when the place of service is 21 (inpatient), 22 (outpatient), or 23 (emergency department), the 7xxxx service will require the modifier –26.

Move slowly through this section, reading all instructions and definitions. If you are confused by words ending in *-gram* or *-graphy*, think of telegram and telegraphy. One is the result, the other the process.

Watch for items requiring modifiers or multiple codes.

Name _____

Radiology–I (70010–73725)

2015 CPT Codes

1. S&I arthrography, left knee _____

2. Thoracic discography, S&I _____

3. X-ray of right knee, four views _____

4. CT of pelvis, with contrast _____

5. Neck CT with and without contrast and additional sections _____

6. Pelvis, two views _____

7. X-ray left eye, no foreign body _____

8. Scoliosis x-ray study of the spine _____

9. Chest x-ray, one view _____

10. Outpatient TMJ arthrography, supervision/interpretation _____

11. Technician administered functional MRI _____

12. Two views right 4th finger _____

13. Cervical MRI, no contrast _____

14. X-ray teeth, right upper, left upper and lower _____

15. Two views cervical spine, outpatient _____

16. Right leg x-ray, 2-month-old baby _____

17. Bilateral fractured ribs, three views _____

18. X-ray left elbow, PA and lateral _____

19. Complete study left hip _____

20. Neck MRI, no contrast, inpatient _____

21. X-ray exam left scapula, three views _____

22. CT thoracic spine with contrast _____

23. Proton imaging for lymph nodes, chest _____

24. X-ray right sialolith _____

25. Cervical myelogram S&I _____

Name _____

Radiology–II (74000–76499)

2015 CPT Codes

1. Upper GI exam with delayed films and KUB _____

2. Bilateral selective adrenal venography, S&I _____

3. Videography of swallowing _____

4. Acute abdomen series _____

5. Cineradiography in operating room _____

6. Bilateral selective adrenal angiography, S&I _____

7. Supervise/interpret voiding urethrocystography _____

8. Bilateral femoral intravascular ultrasound _____

9. Transluminal balloon renal angiography, S&I _____

10. LeVeen shuntogram, S&I _____

11. Barium enema, KUB study _____

12. Contrast monitoring to change percutaneous drain tube, S&I _____

13. S&I retrograde brachial angiography _____

14. Retrograde urography with KUB _____

15. Percutaneous transhepatic portography, S&I, in ER _____

16. S&I, hysterosalpingogram _____

17. Supervise/interpret AV shunt angiogram _____

18. Fluoroscopy, 50 minutes by non operating physician _____

19. Thoracic aortography by serialography, S&I _____

20. Perineogram _____

21. Lymphangiography, right arm, S&I _____

22. Consult/report on x-rays done at University Hospital _____

23. Transhepatic percutaneous cholangiography, S&I _____

24. Follow-up CT study, localized _____

25. Cardiac MRI and stress imaging with and without contrast _____

Radiology–III (76506–79999)

2015 CPT Codes

1.   Complete obstetrical B-scan, 18 weeks, twin pregnancy   _____

2.   Thyroid, metastatic CA imaging, total body, inpatient   _____

3.   Simulation treatment planning, right hip and knee   _____

4.   SPECT cardiac rest and exercise studies at hospital   _____

5.   Lymph gland imaging   _____

6.   Voiding cystogram reflux study with residual bladder study   _____

7.   Radiation treatment: left shoulder and hip, 7.5 MeV (intermediate)   _____

8.   Pulmonary ventilation and perfusion study   _____

9.   Transrectal echo   _____

10.   Intracavitary element placement, 11 ribbons, outpatient   _____

11.   Combined B-12 absorption study   _____

12.   Radioelement placement, surface of left forearm   _____

13.   Ophthalmic biometry A-scan   _____

14.   External hyperthermia, 2.7 cm. deep   _____

15.   Splenic red cell survival measurement   _____

16.   First pass cardiac resting study   _____

17.   Brachytherapy planning, two sources   _____

18.   SPECT bone imaging, professional component only   _____

19.   Radiopharmaceutical treatment via joint infusion   _____

20.   Ultrasound guidance for needle biopsy, S&I   _____

21.   Radiopharmaceutical localization, lung abscess   _____

22.   Neutron radiation, one area   _____

23.   Repeat fetal Doppler echocardiogram   _____

24.   Ultrasound guidance for amniocentesis, S&I   _____

25.   SPECT liver imaging   _____

Pathology and Laboratory

Lab worksheet Part I covers lab panels, drug testing, therapeutic drug assays, evocative/suppression testing, clinical pathology consultations, urinalysis, and ends with chemistry tests. Note that the chemistry tests are listed in alphabetic order.

Part II includes molecular diagnostics, hematology, coagulation, immunology, and tissue typing. CPT 2015 had many changes in Molecular Pathology and Multianalyte Assays, codes 81161–81599, reflecting the new technologies used to detect variants in genes and/or DNA.

The final lab worksheet describes transfusion medicine, microbiology, anatomic pathology, including postmortem examination and cytopathology, cytogenics, surgical pathology, and miscellaneous laboratory services, ending with reproductive medicine procedures.

Reimbursement varies widely for laboratory studies. Review the billing reference manuals for the office testing equipment to determine the correct code for each study.

A federal regulation, the Clinical Laboratory Improvement Act (CLIA), rated laboratory tests by complexity. Each lab is certified to perform a specified level of testing. Some physicians discontinued all office laboratory work. Other practices reduced their laboratory work to only basic, uncomplicated services.

Because many lab tests are expensive, some laboratory order systems show the cost of the test being ordered. This helps the provider decide if the information gained from this study will be worth the cost.

As you complete the worksheets, review the guidelines, and look for instructions within each subsection. A few codes include the physician's services. Watch for the lab tests with legal implications. Unlike the surgical services, the clinical laboratory tests may be numbered so that the lowest code number identifies the most comprehensive study. A few describe testing you can do safely at home.

Some worksheet items require multiple codes or quantity reporting. Watch out for "qualitative" and "quantitative" as some tests have different codes for each study.

Name _____

Pathology and Laboratory–I (80047–83887)

2015 CPT Codes

1. Four studies each, luteinizing hormone and FSH   _____

2. Quantitative theophylline screen, blood   _____

3. Occult blood in stool, three guaiac test cards for neoplasm screen   _____

4. Qualitative cystine/homocystine, urine   _____

5. Urinary amino acids, quantitative, three specimens   _____

6. Glucose tolerance test, four specimens   _____

7. Blood alcohol levels   _____

8. Full sequence analysis BRCA1 and 2   _____

9. Atomic spectroscopy, manganese   _____

10. HDL cholesterol direct measurement   _____

11. Manual microscopic urinalysis   _____

12. Blood catecholamines   _____

13. Creatinine clearance   _____

14. Obstetric panel of tests   _____

15. Hemoglobin, methemoglobin, qualitative   _____

16. Folic acid RBC   _____

17. Cocaine drug screening, qualitative   _____

18. Estriol   _____

19. Color pregnancy test, urine   _____

20. Total serum cholesterol   _____

21. Hepatitis A, B, C antibodies, B surface antigens   _____

22. Fractionation (17-KS) ketosteroids   _____

23. CRH stimulation panel   _____

24. Magnesium screen   _____

25. TSH panel, four studies, 2 hours   _____

_____

Name _____

Pathology and Laboratory–II (83915–86849)

2015 CPT Codes

1. Total blood protein, Western Blot _____

2. Quantitative D-dimer degraded fibrin _____

3. PKU blood test, 2-day-old infant _____

4. Routine prothrombin time _____

5. Vitamin E lab test _____

6. Total T cell with absolute CD4 and CD8 and ratio _____

7. Antibody detection for herpes simplex _____

8. Eastern equine encephalitis antibody test _____

9. Clotting factor VIII, single stage _____

10. Vitamin B-2 analysis _____

11. C-reactive protein _____

12. Parathyroid hormone _____

13. Heparin neutralization _____

14. HLA typing, A, single antigen _____

15. Strip test, urea nitrogen _____

16. Skin test for histoplasmosis _____

17. Chorionic gonadotropin, qualitative _____

18. Hepatitis C antibody _____

19. Total testosterone _____

20. Platelet antibody identification _____

21. Urinary potassium _____

22. Total clotting inhibitor, protein S _____

23. Blood/urine Xylose absorption test _____

24. Rubella antibody screen _____

25. Double-strand DNA antibody _____

Name _____

Pathology and Laboratory–III (86850–89398)

2015 CPT Codes

1. Platelet pooling _____

2. Bone marrow tissue analysis for malignancy _____

3. Diagnostic electron microscopy _____

4. Stool culture for *Salmonella* _____

5. Coroner ordered autopsy _____

6. Surgical pathology, gross/micro, uterus with tubes and ovaries with tumor _____

7. Flow cytometry, DNA analysis _____

8. Rabbit inoculation, observation, and dissection _____

9. Influenza detection by immunoassay _____

10. Gross autopsy, including brain _____

11. Surgical pathology, gross/micro cholesteatoma _____

12. Preoperative autologous blood collection/storage prior to elective surgery _____

13. Motility, volume and count semen analysis _____

14. Consult/report on slides from University Hospital _____

15. Antimicrobial sensitivity study, 10 disks _____

16. Chlamydia culture _____

17. Limited chromosome analysis/banding, amniotic fluid _____

18. KOH skin slide prep _____

19. Forensic cytopathology for sperm _____

20. CSF cell count with differential _____

21. Thawing fresh frozen plasma, two units _____

22. Immunofluorescent detection Type 1 herpes _____

23. HIV-1 antigens with HIV-1 and HIV-2 antibodies _____

24. Collection of vaginal smear for dark field exam _____

25. Intraoperative consultation and frozen section, two specimens _____

Medicine

Worksheet I covers injections, psychiatry, dialysis services, diagnostic medical services for gastroenterology, and nonsurgical procedures on the eye and ear.

Worksheet II has cardiovascular and pulmonary diagnostic and therapeutic services, procedures for allergy, and neurology.

Worksheet III includes genetics, chemotherapy, and physical medicine. The special services of osteopaths and chiropractors, additional anesthesia codes, and other special procedures and services are the final subsections of CPT. The Category II and III codes may not be accepted by all insurance plans. Some of the special services, procedures, and reports also may be excluded from payment.

Many CPTs ago, office visits were part of the Medicine section. Then they became E/M services and are now listed separately. The invasive procedures in this section are diagnostic and are usually considered nonsurgical. This may seem strange since coronary angioplasty, the procedure some people have instead of open-heart surgery, is in this section.

Many doctors use services from this section, such as injections, EKGs, and pulmonary function testing. Generally, as you can see from the subsection listing, these services belong to a medical specialty. Study these services carefully. The guidelines for this section should be familiar. Now we apply them to medical services rather than surgery.

Caution: Watch for multiple codes, modifiers, and quantity reporting. One item requires a code from the E/M section.

Medicine–I (90281–92700)

2015 CPT Codes

1. Anterior endothelial microscopy, cell count, photo/report   _____

2. Medical hypnotherapy to stop smoking   _____

3. One mini IM dose Rho(D)   _____

4. Tinnitus assessment, right ear   _____

5. Rhinomanometry   _____

6. Binaural hearing aid exam   _____

7. Manometric studies, anus and rectum   _____

8. Bernstein test for esophagitis   _____

9. Tangent screen visual fields, right eye   _____

10. Supply Tetanus vaccine for use with jet injector, 27-year-old male   _____

11. Hepatitis B immunization series, first visit, 19-year-old dialysis patient (four-dose schedule)   _____

12. Biofeedback training for arrhythmia   _____

13. Monthly dialysis monitoring, 16-year-old female, one visit   _____

14. Insight-oriented psychotherapy, 1 hour and 5 minutes, in the office   _____

15. Psychotherapy with family, patient absent   _____

16. Comprehensive eye exam, new patient   _____

17. Fluorescein multiframe angiography, complete   _____

18. Contact lens replacement, right   _____

19. Impedance tympanometry   _____

20. Start of dialysis training, one session   _____

21. Air audiometry   _____

22. Fitting of bifocal lenses   _____

23. Electroconvulsive treatment, one session, for seizures   _____

24. Audiometry by select picture   _____

25. Psychotherapy session with patient and family, 60 minutes   _____

Medicine–II (92920–96020)

2015 CPT Codes

1. Coronary thrombolysis by IV infusion _____

2. Inpatient right and left heart catheterization, congenital heart defect _____

3. Interpretation/report only, tilt table cardiac testing _____

4. Balloon angioplasty (PTCA) with insertion of drug-eluting stent in coronary artery. _____

5. EMG cranial nerve supplied muscles, bilateral _____

6. Dispense 15 doses antigen, bee and wasp _____

7. Brief study, transcranial Doppler _____

8. Cardiac stress test, tracing only _____

9. Awake/sleep EEG, 10 p.m. to 7 a.m. _____

10. Initiation and management of CPAP _____

11. Scratch tests, 10 trees, three venom _____

12. Electromyography, 10 muscles, while running on treadmill _____

13. Twenty-four-hour ECG, recording only _____

14. Complete service, 1 month patient activated spirometry recording _____

15. Repeat analysis of cranial nerve stimulator implant _____

16. Cholinesterase inhibitor challenge test for myasthenia gravis _____

17. His Bundle recording _____

18. Complete four extremity plethysmography _____

19. Venous Doppler, both legs, complete study _____

20. Transesophageal echocardiogram, total service _____

21. Ear oximetry for O_2 saturation _____

22. S&I for ventricular angiography during left heart cath _____

23. Stress echocardiogram, complete _____

24. Complete ambulatory blood pressure monitoring, 32 hours _____

25. Electrical testing of blink reflex _____

Medicine–III (96040 and Category II and III codes)

2015 CPT Codes

1. Nurse visit to patient's home for urinary catheter change _____

2. Nurse supervision of hyperbaric oxygen therapy for a patient experiencing carbon monoxide poisoning _____

3. Iontophoresis, 30 minutes _____

4. Limited developmental testing with interpretation report _____

5. Osteopathic manipulative treatment (OMT), head and neck _____

6. IV conscious sedation, 30 minutes, 67-year-old male, for esophageal dilation _____

7. Phone evaluation, 25 minutes with suicidal patient who just returned from 2 months in Europe _____

8. Acupuncture, four needles _____

9. Documented assessment for risk of falls _____

10. Breath test for rejection of heart transplant _____

11. Telogen/antigen counts on hair clipped at the lab _____

12. Assessment to determine suicide risk _____

13. Behavior intervention, 30 minutes, twins and both parents _____

14. Three hours medical testimony _____

15. Initial nurse visit for infant born at home _____

16. Use of whirlpool and scalpel wound debridement, 14.5 sq. cm. _____

17. Reevaluation of physical therapy treatment _____

18. Diabetic meal planning education, one hour, four patients _____

19. Home visit and enema for fecal impaction _____

20. Patient education/counseling, prescribed beta-blocker medication _____

21. Chemotherapy, arterial infusion, 55 minutes _____

22. Gait and stairs retraining, 30 minutes _____

23. IM chemotherapy administration _____

24. Chiropractic treatment, lumbar and sacral spinal areas _____

25. Home visit infusion, 5-year-old male hemophiliac, 1.5 hours. _____

UNIT III HCPCS LEVEL II CODES

Developed by the federal government, HCPCS (Healthcare Common Procedure Coding System) National Level II codes identify over 5,000 codes and descriptive terminology for services not included in CPT. HCPCS provides codes for reporting supplies, injectables, and the services of nonphysician providers such as ambulance companies and Medicaid programs. HCPCS code changes start on January 1 with the new CPT codes.

Level II HCPCS codes begin with a letter followed by four digits. Although the codes were originally designed for Medicare and Medicaid, they are part of the HIPAA-designated code sets and most private insurers accept and understand them. Medicare, Medicaid, and some other payers may require the provider to register as a Durable Medical Equipment (DME) supplier before payment can be made for some supplies and equipment.

HCPCS lists codes alphabetically. Some Level II sections are unusual. D (dental) codes were eliminated in 2012 at the request of the American Dental Association. K codes are used only by Durable Medical Equipment Medicare Administrative Contractors (DME MACs) and are temporary codes. Many M (medical) services eventually appear in CPT so this list changes each year. Q codes are temporary codes, sometimes appearing mid-year when it becomes necessary to identify a service previously included in or reported by another code. Medicare and Medicaid bulletins will tell you when to report a new Q code. S codes may be used by the Blues, Medicaid, and commercial payers to facilitate claims processing and are not valid for the Medicare program. Medicaid programs asked for the inclusion of the T codes that may also be used by private insurers, but never for Medicare.

Read the introduction for an explanation of the HCPCS reference. Each of the sections begins with guidelines on how to use the codes correctly. There may be a mini-index to that section. The HCPCS index may show a single code, a range of codes, or provide no listing for that service. Like the CPT index, you may need to think of other ways to describe the service if you are to find the correct code.

HCPCS modifiers appear in the appendix or near the front or back of the book. Another appendix contains a summary of code changes. A different appendix has a list of modified or deleted codes. There are two sorted lists in HCPCS, a table of drugs, and a general index. Many private companies print versions of this codebook. Your reference may have numbers or letters to identify each appendix, or differ in format, but the codes and descriptions should be consistent with all vendors. These companies may also provide an expanded index or additional information on the use of these codes.

As you code the worksheet, start with the index. Then verify the code(s) with the actual code section as there may be sizes, quantities, or other variables in selecting the correct code. Read the guidelines to be certain you select the proper code. Many terms are similar and may be unfamiliar. If you use these codes in your work, consult with your employer to be certain you report the correct code.

HCPCS has special alphanumeric or two-letter modifiers. Some of these are included in the Modifier worksheet.

Name _____

HCPCS Level II Codes

2015 HCPCS

1.   Delivery of monaural behind-the-ear hearing aid   _____

2.   Medicaid case management, 1 month   _____

3.   Injection, 100,000 units of Bicillin CR   _____

4.   Premolded removable metatarsal support, right foot   _____

5.   Chelation therapy   _____

6.   Annual wellness assessment by a nurse practitioner   _____

7.   Right shoe modified with outside sole wedge   _____

8.   Dispensed 60 days of prenatal vitamins   _____

9.   Injection, 8 mg Compazine   _____

10. Preschool screening for language problems   _____

11. Vinyl urinary bag with tube and leg strap   _____

12. Custom made plastic artificial eye   _____

13. Obtained Pap smear, sent to lab   _____

14. Methotrexate, 50 mg   _____

15. Non-emergency transportation by wheelchair van   _____

16. Nasogastric tubing, no stylet   _____

17. Adjustable aluminum three-prong cane, with tips   _____

18. Non-sterile dialysis gloves, one box of 100   _____

19. Mitomycin, 5 mg injected   _____

20. Took x-ray machine to nursing home, one patient seen   _____

21. Lift assist for elbow   _____

22. Injection, Estradiol, 9 mg   _____

23. Needleless injection device   _____

24. Toronto orthosis for Legg Perthes disease   _____

25. Recording apnea monitor, high-risk infant   _____

Current Procedural Terminology ©2014 American Medical Association. All Rights Reserved.

Modifiers

Modifiers are two-character suffixes for procedure codes. They provide important information on how that service changed in some way without altering the definition of the code. Using modifiers properly eliminates some of the need to send procedure notes with claims. All CPT modifiers are two-digit numbers, and HCPCS modifiers are two letters or a letter and digit. Some modifiers apply to evaluation and management services only while others clarify surgical procedures. Both CPT and HCPCS provide a complete list of modifiers in an appendix.

CPT modifiers may indicate a reduced or expanded service, bilateral procedures, or the professional component of a service. HCPCS modifiers may indicate the rental or purchase of a piece of equipment, services by a social worker, or the services that are provided in a medically underserved area. Medicare and Medicaid may also direct you to apply HCPCS modifiers to CPT codes. Like the codes they modify, modifiers may be changed or eliminated with each new edition of CPT and HCPCS.

Modifiers may be shown as –22 or –AN. The "–" is not reported but is useful if you write out a code as "12345–22" or "54321–LT." The claim form and computer files have special columns or fields for modifiers. Some payers may ask you to report modifiers as a five-character code, 09922 or 099LT.

The worksheet requires a modifier for each scenario. Use the appendix in the CPT and HCPCS codebooks to select the correct two-character modifier. Some items may require multiple answers.

Name _____

Modifiers

2015 CPT

1. The patient had major surgery by Dr. Jones on July 16 and saw the doctor on August 4 for an unrelated office visit. The August 4 service requires modifier: _____

2. Dr. Rodriquez asks Dr. White to assist at a major surgery because a surgery resident is not available. Dr. White reports the surgery code with modifier: _____

3. When an insurer requires a presurgical second opinion, the service is reported with the modifier: _____

4. The surgery was difficult because the patient was a paraplegic weighing 427 pounds. To report these circumstances to the insurer, use modifier: _____

5. Dr. Dinn, the family doctor, asks a surgeon, Dr. Green, to see the patient at City Hospital as she may need surgery. Dr. Green schedules the surgery for tomorrow and reports today's service with modifier: _____

6. Dr. Schneider does an appendectomy and removes a mole from the patient's neck while in the OR. Use modifier ____ on the ____ service line of the claim form (according to payer instructions).   _____

2015 HCPCS

1. Dr. Reed, a clinical psychologist, saw a Medicare patient for diagnostic testing. Dr. Reed reports the service with modifier: _____

2. If you refile a claim and change the procedure code because it was incorrect on the original claim, use modifier: _____

3. When a procedure is recorded and stored on an analog tape recorder, use modifier QT. For a digital recording, use: _____

4. Dr. Johns owns the portable x-ray equipment, but Dr. Armando does the interpretation and report. Identify the modifiers for both doctors: _____

5. Dr. Little sees patients in an inner-city clinic designated as a physician scarcity area. He receives additional compensation for these services by reporting modifier: _____

6. Mr. Blevins obtains a cane from the medical supply store. If it was a new cane, report modifier for new equipment: _____

UNIT IV ICD-10-CM

Introduction to ICD-10-CM

Diagnosis coding systems are older than procedure coding methods. More than 100 years ago a French physician developed a system for coding causes of death. In the early 1900s, the U.S. Public Health Service (PHS) began using the same codes. The World Health Organization (WHO) developed ICD in the late 1930s. In 1950, the PHS and the Veterans Administration (VA) adopted ICDA-8, the *International Classification of Diseases, Eighth Revision, Adapted.* With the U.S. implementation of ICDA-8 (ICD Adapted), our information on mortality and morbidity could be matched with statistics from the rest of the world.

Nongovernmental hospitals began to use ICDA-8, and the PHS expanded the system to include codes for surgery and treatment. In 1979, the government mandated the use of a new system, ICD-9-CM, for reporting services to Medicare and Medicaid and later extended to all payers by the Health Insurance Portability and Accountability Act (HIPAA).

The ICD-9-CM, *International Classification of Diseases, Ninth Revision, Clinical Modification*, was compatible with the WHO system, ICD-9. Congress required a standardized coding system for the implementation of Diagnosis Related Groups (DRGs), in 1983. The DRGs became part of Medicare's hospital inpatient payment method. All the diagnoses in ICD-9-CM were grouped into categories based on resource attributes. The hospital received payment for the inpatient's DRG category, not the cost of the patient's care. In 2007, another expanded version of the DRG system was developed called MS-DRGs (Medicare Severity DRGs), which incorporated levels of severity within the reimbursement method.

After the government standardized the diagnosis coding system, many private organizations started printing the books with improvements. Some placed a color-coded box over the numbers that need a fourth or fifth digit; some distributed the codes in a ring binder; others had anatomical drawings throughout to illustrate the codes. The government maintained the codes but no longer printed an annual edition of ICD-9-CM. However, the government does warn that it is not responsible for the errors made by others in printing the codes.

ICD-9-CM updated codes quarterly, but if the office bought a new book each August, it should be safe to use for the next year. The publishers print the year prominently on the cover so you know when the book becomes obsolete. It seems likely that the 2015 edition of ICD-9-CM will be the last one published now that ICD-10-CM will soon become the diagnosis coding system.

Many physicians' offices have used only 50 to 100 diagnosis codes. Rather than look them up each time, codes appear on encounter forms or "cheat sheets" used by the billers. There are two problems with this approach. First, the list restricts the number of diagnoses available. Do all the patients have only two or three kinds of anemia?

The worksheets contain columns for both ICD-10-CM and for ICD-9-CM. You will need access to a current draft of ICD-10-CM code book to complete these exercises.

Using ICD-10-CM

The physician's office and outpatient settings report the primary diagnosis that explains the reason for the visit. This diagnosis supports the medical necessity; it is the reason services were provided. In the hospital inpatient setting, the principal diagnosis is reported. The principal diagnosis is the condition after study to be chiefly responsible for the admission of the patient to the hospital. Suppose a physician sees a patient complaining of abdominal pain. If you can establish the cause, such as acute appendicitis, you may report that code. If the complaints are vague, maybe the flu, the threat of layoffs at work, or an upcoming week of final exams the doctor may code "abdominal pain" for the office visit.

As you do with CPT, you will need to become familiar with the diagnosis coding conventions. Conventions and the Official Coding Guidelines support consistency and accurate use of ICD-9-CM and ICD-10-CM. Before beginning the worksheets, take time to review the introduction, the terminology, and the format of the alphabetic and tabular indexes. Also, pay careful attention to the ICD-10-CM Official Guidelines for Coding and Reporting and the chapter-specific coding guidelines.

Diagnosis Coding—Quick and Dirty

The ICD classification system was developed to collect information worldwide on the presence of disease. In the United States, the ICD-9-CM (soon to replaced with ICD-10-CM) classification system is also used for claims processing. The ICD code explains the reason the patient is seeking care and the CPT code describes the services.

Diagnosis codes must be reasonable for the service performed. Always subject your coding to a reasonableness test, which is the subject of the next section called Medical Necessity.

Medical Necessity

Medicare (and other payers) pays for medical services and supplies that are "reasonable and necessary" and/or appropriate based on the diagnosis reported with ICD-9-CM. Coverage criteria are outlined in policies developed by Medicare called National Coverage Determinations (NCDs), or by the local Medicare carrier policies referred to as Local Coverage Determinations (LCD). For example, it would not be reasonable or necessary for a patient to receive an x-ray of the foot if the diagnosis is coded for a fractured wrist. Note the following list of ICD-10-CM code ranges and CPT procedure categories. This list will be referenced for the Medical Necessity Exercise.

	Diagnoses	Description		Procedures	Description
1.	A00–B99	Infectious/Parasitic Disease	1.	99201–99499	Evaluation/Management
2.	C00–D49	Neoplasms	2.	00100–01999	Anesthesia
3.	D50–D89	Blood/Blood-Forming/Immune	3.	10021–19499	Integumentary System
4.	E00–E89	Endocrine/Metabolic Diseases	4.	20005–29999	Musculoskeletal System
5.	F01–F99	Mental/Behavior Disorders	5.	30000–32999	Respiratory System
6.	G00–G99	Nervous System	6.	33010–37799	Cardiovascular System
7.	H00–H59	Diseases Eye/Adnexa	7.	38100–39599	Hemic/Lymph/Mediastinum
8.	H60–H95	Diseases Ear/Mastoid	8.	40490–49999	Digestive System
9.	I00–I99	Circulatory System	9.	50010–53899	Urinary System
10.	J00–J99	Respiratory System	10.	54000–55980	Male Genital/Intersex
11.	K00–K99	Digestive System	11.	56405–59899	Female/Maternity
12.	L00–L99	Skin/Subcutaneous Tissue	12.	60000–64999	Endocrine/Nervous Systems
13.	M00–M99	Musculoskeletal/Connective Tissue	13.	65091–68899	Eye/Ocular Adnexa
14.	N00–N99	Genitourinary System	14.	69000–69990	Auditory System
15.	O00–O99	Pregnancy/Childbirth/Puerperium	15.	70010–79999	Radiology Services
16.	P00–P96	Conditions Perinatal Period	16.	80047–89398	Pathology Services
17.	Q00–Q99	Congenital Malformations	17.	90281–99607	Medical Services
18.	R00–R99	Signs/Symptoms	18.	0001F–0339T	Category II and III Codes
19.	S00–T88	Injury/Poisoning/External causes			
20.	V00–Y99	Morbidity Causes			
21.	Z00–Z99	Health Status/Services			

Name _____

Medical Necessity Exercise

1. A patient was diagnosed with epididymitis and requires surgical intervention. Which CPT code range section is most likely to be reported for this surgery?

   a. Respiratory

   b. Digestive System

   c. Urinary System

   d. Male Genital/Intersex

2. The surgeon performed a diagnostic amniocentesis and CPT code 59000 was reported. The diagnosis to support medical necessity would most likely be reported from what ICD-10-CM range of codes?

   a. A00–B99

   b. D50–D89

   c. O00–O99

   d. S00–T88

3. A patient was diagnosed with cholesteatoma and required surgical intervention. Medical necessity for the surgery would be supported from what code range in CPT?

   a. Integumentary System

   b. Respiratory System

   c. Digestive System

   d. Auditory System

4. As a result of a traumatic fracture, the surgeon performed an open reduction with internal fixation (ORIF) of a fractured femur (CPT code 27269). The diagnosis code to support medical necessity would be reported from which of the following chapters?

   a. Musculoskeletal/Connective Tissue

   b. Injury/Poisoning/External causes

   c. Signs/Symptoms

   d. Congenital Malformations

5. Which of the following scenarios does not support medical necessity?

   a. Diagnosis of gangrene for a patient with CPT code for amputation of the toe

   b. Diagnosis of adenocarcinoma of the lung with CPT code for pneumonectomy

   c. Diagnosis of severe osteomyelitis with CPT code for percutaneous skeletal fixation

   d. Diagnosis of morbid obesity with CPT code for Roux-en-Y anastomosis

ICD-10-CM Official Guidelines for Coding and Reporting

Section IV. Diagnostic Coding and Reporting Guidelines for Outpatient Services

These coding guidelines for outpatient diagnoses have been approved for use by hospitals/ providers in coding and reporting hospital-based outpatient services and provider-based office visits.

Information about the use of certain abbreviations, punctuation, symbols, and other conventions used in the ICD-10-CM Tabular List (code numbers and titles), can be found in Section IA of these guidelines, under "Conventions Used in the Tabular List." Section I.B. contains general guidelines that apply to the entire classification. Section I.C. contains chapter-specific guidelines that correspond to the chapters as they are arranged in the classification. Information about the correct sequence to use in finding a code is also described in Section I.

The terms encounter and visit are often used interchangeably in describing outpatient service contacts and, therefore, appear together in these guidelines without distinguishing one from the other.

Though the conventions and general guidelines apply to all settings, coding guidelines for outpatient and provider reporting of diagnoses will vary in a number of instances from those for inpatient diagnoses, recognizing that:

> The Uniform Hospital Discharge Data Set (UHDDS) definition of principal diagnosis applies only to inpatients in acute, short-term, long-term care and psychiatric hospitals.

> Coding guidelines for inconclusive diagnoses (probable, suspected, rule out, etc.) were developed for inpatient reporting and do not apply to outpatients.

A. Selection of first-listed condition

> In the outpatient setting, the term first-listed diagnosis is used in lieu of principal diagnosis.

ICD-10-CM Official Guidelines for Coding and Reporting

In determining the first-listed diagnosis the coding conventions of ICD-10-CM, as well as the general and disease specific guidelines take precedence over the outpatient guidelines.

Diagnoses often are not established at the time of the initial encounter/visit. It may take two or more visits before the diagnosis is confirmed.

The most critical rule involves beginning the search for the correct code assignment through the Alphabetic Index. Never begin searching initially in the Tabular List as this will lead to coding errors.

1. **Outpatient Surgery**

When a patient presents for outpatient surgery (same day surgery), code the reason for the surgery as the first-listed diagnosis (reason for the encounter), even if the surgery is not performed due to a contraindication.

2. **Observation Stay**

When a patient is admitted for observation for a medical condition, assign a code for the medical condition as the first-listed diagnosis. When a patient presents for outpatient surgery and develops complications requiring admission to observation, code the reason for the surgery as the first reported diagnosis (reason for the encounter), followed by codes for the complications as secondary diagnoses.

B. Codes from A00.0 through T88.9, Z00-Z99

The appropriate code(s) from A00.0 through T88.9, Z00-Z99 must be used to identify diagnoses, symptoms, conditions, problems, complaints, or other reason(s) for the encounter/visit.

C. Accurate reporting of ICD-10-CM diagnosis codes

For accurate reporting of ICD-10-CM diagnosis codes, the documentation should describe the patient's condition, using terminology which includes specific diagnoses as well as symptoms, problems, or reasons for the encounter. There are ICD-10-CM codes to describe all of these. ICD-10-CM Official Guidelines for Coding and Reporting FY 2015

D. Codes that describe symptoms and signs

Codes that describe symptoms and signs, as opposed to diagnoses, are acceptable for reporting purposes when a diagnosis has not been established (confirmed) by the provider. Chapter 18 of ICD-10-CM, Symptoms, Signs, and Abnormal Clinical and Laboratory Findings Not Elsewhere Classified (codes R00-R99) contain many, but not all codes for symptoms.

ICD-10-CM Official Guidelines for Coding and Reporting

E. Encounters for circumstances other than a disease or injury

ICD-10-CM provides codes to deal with encounters for circumstances other than a disease or injury. The Factors Influencing Health Status and Contact with Health Services codes (Z00-Z99) are provided to deal with occasions when circumstances other than a disease or injury are recorded as diagnosis or problems.
See Section I.C.21. Factors influencing health status and contact with health services.

F. Level of Detail in Coding

1. ICD-10-CM codes with 3, 4, 5, 6 or 7 characters

ICD-10-CM is composed of codes with 3, 4, 5, 6 or 7 characters. Codes with three characters are included in ICD-10-CM as the heading of a category of codes that may be further subdivided by the use of fourth, fifth, sixth or seventh characters to provide greater specificity.

2. Use of full number of *characters* required for a code

A three-character code is to be used only if it is not further subdivided. A code is invalid if it has not been coded to the full number of characters required for that code, including the 7th character, if applicable.

G. ICD-10-CM code for the diagnosis, condition, problem, or other reason for encounter/visit

List first the ICD-10-CM code for the diagnosis, condition, problem, or other reason for encounter/visit shown in the medical record to be chiefly responsible for the services provided. List additional codes that describe any coexisting conditions. In some cases the first-listed diagnosis may be a symptom when a diagnosis has not been established (confirmed) by the physician.

H. Uncertain diagnosis

Do not code diagnoses documented as "probable," "suspected," "questionable," "rule out," or "working diagnosis" or other similar terms indicating uncertainty. Rather, code the condition(s) to the highest degree of certainty for that encounter/ visit, such as symptoms, signs, abnormal test results, or other reason for the visit. Please note: This differs from the coding practices used by short-term, acute care, long-term care and psychiatric hospitals. ICD-10-CM Official Guidelines for Coding and Reporting FY 2015.

I. Chronic diseases

Chronic diseases treated on an ongoing basis may be coded and reported as many times as the patient receives treatment and care for the condition(s).

ICD-10-CM Official Guidelines for Coding and Reporting

J. Code all documented conditions that coexist

Code all documented conditions that coexist at the time of the encounter/visit, and require or affect patient care treatment or management. Do not code conditions that were previously treated and no longer exist. However, history codes (categories Z80- Z87) may be used as secondary codes if the historical condition or family history has an impact on current care or influences treatment.

K. Patients receiving diagnostic services only

For patients receiving diagnostic services only during an encounter/visit, sequence first the diagnosis, condition, problem, or other reason for encounter/visit shown in the medical record to be chiefly responsible for the outpatient services provided during the encounter/visit. Codes for other diagnoses (e.g., chronic conditions) may be sequenced as additional diagnoses.

For encounters for routine laboratory/radiology testing in the absence of any signs, symptoms, or associated diagnosis, assign Z01.89, Encounter for other specified special examinations. If routine testing is performed during the same encounter as a test to evaluate a sign, symptom, or diagnosis, it is appropriate to assign both the Z code and the code describing the reason for the non-routine test.

For outpatient encounters for diagnostic tests that have been interpreted by a physician, and the final report is available at the time of coding, code any confirmed or definitive diagnosis(es) documented in the interpretation. Do not code related signs and symptoms as additional diagnoses.

Please note: This differs from the coding practice in the hospital inpatient setting regarding abnormal findings on test results.

L. Patients receiving therapeutic services only

For patients receiving therapeutic services only during an encounter/visit, sequence first the diagnosis, condition, problem, or other reason for encounter/visit shown in the medical record to be chiefly responsible for the outpatient services provided during the encounter/visit. Codes for other diagnoses (e.g., chronic conditions) may be sequenced as additional diagnoses.

The only exception to this rule is that when the primary reason for the admission/encounter is chemotherapy or radiation therapy, the appropriate Z code for the service is listed first, and the diagnosis or problem for which the service is being performed listed second.

M. Patients receiving preoperative evaluations only

For patients receiving preoperative evaluations only, sequence first a code from subcategory Z01.81, Encounter for pre-procedural examinations, to describe the pre-op consultations. Assign a code for the condition to describe the reason for the surgery as an additional diagnosis. Code also any findings related to the pre-op evaluation.

ICD-10-CM Official Guidelines for Coding and Reporting

N. Ambulatory surgery

For ambulatory surgery, code the diagnosis for which the surgery was performed. If the postoperative diagnosis is known to be different from the preoperative diagnosis at the time the diagnosis is confirmed, select the postoperative diagnosis for coding, since it is the most definitive.

O. Routine outpatient prenatal visits

See Section I.C.15. Routine outpatient prenatal visits.

P. Encounters for general medical examinations with abnormal findings

The subcategories for encounters for general medical examinations, Z00.0-, provide codes for with and without abnormal findings. Should a general medical examination result in an abnormal finding, the code for general medical examination with abnormal finding should be assigned as the first-listed diagnosis. A secondary code for the abnormal finding should also be coded.

Q. Encounters for routine health screenings

See Section I.C.21. Factors influencing health status and contact with health services, Screening.

ICD-10-CM Official Guidelines for Coding and Reporting FY 2015

Courtesy of the Centers for Medicare & Medicaid Services, www.cms.hhs.gov

Moving from the old ICD-9-CM to the new ICD-10-CM

In the near future, health care providers using ICD-9-CM must begin reporting diagnoses from ICD-10-CM. This change requires project plans that include education and systems analysis. The Centers for Medicare and Medicaid Services (CMS) has developed a Web site devoted to helping physician practices transition to ICD-10-CM. The interactive Web site allows practices to build an action plan based on their medical speciality. Perform a Web search to access the site, called Road to 10, and examine the resources more closely.

ICD-10-CM has over 69,000 codes; ICD-9-CM has fewer than 15,000 codes. ICD-10-CM has 21 chapters; ICD-9-CM has 19 chapters. ICD-10-CM codes are all alphanumeric; ICD-9-CM has only numeric codes except for the E and V codes. ICD-10-CM codes are three to seven characters in length; ICD-9-CM codes are three to five characters long.

If you presently code from ICD-9-CM for diagnoses and CPT for procedures, you will continue to use CPT with ICD-10-CM. If you currently code from ICD-9-CM Volume 3 (Procedures), you will use ICD-10-PCS. ICD-10-PCS is replacing Volume 3 of ICD-9-CM and CMS is only requiring ICD-10-PCS for hospital inpatients.

CMS announced a partial freeze on code changes prior to the implementation of ICD-10-CM. Code changes will be made only to capture new technology and new diseases.

ICD-10-CM has guidelines for reporting but the rules are more complex than the guidelines of ICD-9-CM. The coder will need a greater understanding of anatomy, physiology, and terminology to code correctly in ICD-10-CM. These guideline sections are as follows:

Section I: Conventions, general coding guidelines, and chapter-specific guidelines

Section II: Selection of principal diagnosis

Section III: Reporting additional diagnoses

Section IV: Diagnostic coding and reporting guidelines for outpatient services

Generally, Sections II and III are used for hospital reporting. Sections I and IV will be used most frequently by the physician's office coder.

There are significant notes at the start of each chapter in ICD-10-CM specifying how those codes are to be used. These instructions clarify many scenarios that have caused problems for coders over the years. While ICD-10-CM requires more precise coding, we are given additional directions for selecting the correct code.

Each chapter begins with information on what is included, what codes are never reported together (Excludes 1), and the conditions that are not included in the code but may be reported with that code if both conditions exist (Excludes 2). There's also a breakdown of the code blocks in that chapter, such as:

| D00–D09 | In situ neoplasms | P10–P15 | Birth trauma | V00–X58 | Accidents |
| K40–K46 | Hernia | S80–S89 | Injuries to the knee and lower leg | X92–Y08 | Assault |

The following table compares ICD-10-CM chapters with the chapters in ICD-9-CM:

ICD-10-CM Chapter/Name	Code Range	ICD-9-CM Chapter/Name	Code Range
1. Certain Infectious and Parasitic Diseases	A00–B99	1. Infectious and Parasitic Diseases	001–139
2. Neoplasms	C00–D49	2. Neoplasms	140–239
3. Diseases of the Blood and Blood-forming Organs and Certain Disorders Involving the Immune Mechanism	D50–D89	3. Endocrine, Nutritional, and Metabolic Diseases, and Immunity Disorders	240–279
4. Endocrine, Nutritional, and Metabolic Diseases	E00–E89	4. Disease of Blood and Blood-forming Organs	280–289
5. Mental and Behavioral Disorders	F01–F99	5. Mental Disorders	290–319
6. Diseases of the Nervous System	G00–G99	6. Diseases of the Nervous System and Sense Organs	320–389
7. Diseases of the Eye and Adnexa	H00–H59	7. Diseases of the Circulatory System	390–459
8. Diseases of the Ear and Mastoid Process	H60–H95	8. Diseases of the Respiratory System	460–519
9. Diseases of the Circulatory System	I00–I99	9. Diseases of the Digestive System	520–579
10. Disease of the Respiratory System	J00–J99	10. Diseases of the Genitourinary System	580–629
11. Diseases of the Digestive System	K00–K94	11. Complications of Pregnancy, Childbirth, and the Puerperium	630–679
12. Diseases of the Skin and Subcutaneous Tissue	L00–L99	12. Diseases of the Skin and Subcutaneous Tissue	680–709
13. Diseases of the Musculoskeletal System and Connective Tissue	M00–M99	13. Diseases of the Musculoskeletal System and Connective Tissue	710–739
14. Diseases of the Genitourinary System	N00–N99	14. Congenital Anomalies	740–759
15. Pregnancy, Childbirth, and the Puerperium	O00–O99	15. Certain Conditions Originating in the Perinatal Period	760–779
16. Certain Conditions Originating in the Perinatal Period	P00–P96	16. Signs, Symptoms, and Ill-Defined Conditions	780–799
17. Congenital Malformations, Deformations, and Chromosomal Abnormalities	Q00–Q99	17. Injury and Poisoning	800–999
18. Symptoms, Signs, and Abnormal Clinical and Laboratory Findings, Not Elsewhere Classified	R00–R99	18. Classification of Factors Influencing Health Status and Contact with Health Service	V01–V91
19. Injury, Poisoning, and Certain Other Consequences of External Causes	S00–T88	19. Supplemental Classification of External Causes of Injury and Poisoning	E000–E999
20. External Causes of Morbidity	V00–Y99		
21. Factors Influencing Health Status and Contact with Health Services	Z00–Z99		

© Cengage Learning®

ICD-10-CM codes are structured as follows:

Character	1	Alpha, except "U"
	2	Numeric
	3	Alpha or numeric (not case sensitive)
	4–7	Alpha or numeric (not case sensitive; may have an "x" as a place holder in positions 4–6)

ICD-10-CM uses all letters except "U" as the first character. The code will be invalid if the x's are omitted. All codes requiring a seventh character must include an x or xx unless the code is already six characters in length. The seventh character of the code gives specific information about the encounter or the medical condition. It must appear in the seventh position. The x is a placeholder to allow for the proper number of characters. The use of seventh characters are throughout the classification system. However, the majority of the seventh characters appear in Obstetrics and Injuries and Poisonings.

The seventh character may indicate that this is an initial encounter for this condition (A), that this is a subsequent encounter for fracture with delayed healing (G), or that this encounter is for the sequela of a condition (S). If this key information appears in any other position but the seventh, important data will be missing and therefore the code will be invalid. Code S82 ("fracture of the lower leg, including ankle") has 16 different letters for the seventh position. There are also notes stating that some of the 16 characters do not apply to certain subcategories of S82 (see "fracture of the patella," S82.0).

Since the place holder is not case sensitive, you may wish to use lower case for readability, as these are complex code configurations:

S61.022A	Initial encounter for a laceration with foreign body of left thumb without damage to nail
S77.02xA	Initial encounter for a crushing injury to the left hip
Y36.6x0S	Sequelae of war operations involving biological weapons encountered as a military personnel

Computer systems convert lower case letters to upper case for health care claims. If you haven't stopped using the lower case L for 1 (one) or continue to use the capital O for the number 0 (zero), get out of that habit now as this will create invalid codes when reporting in ICD-10-CM.

Organizations are introducing special references and online courses to provide a greater understanding of anatomy, physiology, and terminology described and used in ICD-10-CM. These may be especially helpful if you code from operative reports where the physician's terminology may not match the terms used in the coding system.

This material was prepared with the 2015 draft of ICD-10-CM. The final printed copy of ICD-10-CM may not be released before the implementation date, but CMS electronic files will have the most current edition.

Assignment of ICD-10-CM codes, just like ICD-9-CM, must be supported by documentation. One of the key features of ICD-10-CM is the ability to report laterality (left, right). The diagnosis code should correspond to the CPT procedure code when reporting laterality. Note the example below.

Coding Conflicts

The goal for reporting codes on a claim form is to have "clean claims" with no coding conflicts, which meet medical necessity and are reflective of the documentation in the health record. The changes in ICD-10-CM codes highlight the need to closely audit the possibility of a conflict, such as with the following example:

Example: The physician documents the diagnosis as chalazion of the right upper eyelid requiring an excision.

Procedure:	Excise chalazion, right upper lid: CPT code 67800-E3
ICD-10-CM:	H00.11: Chalazion, right upper eyelid
	H00.12: Chalazion, right lower eyelid
	H00.13: Chalazion, right eye, unspecified eyelid
	H00.14: Chalazion, left upper eyelid
	H00.15: Chalazion, left lower eyelid
	H00.16: Chalazion, left eye, unspecified eyelid
	H00.19: Chalazion, unspecified eye, unspecified eyelid

All these are incorrect diagnoses except H00.11. Let's hope our medical record documentation never results in having to select H00.19.

Will claims be rejected when we report a second initial encounter for the same condition reported last week? Will there be problems from reporting too many "unspecified" diagnoses? If we report an external cause code at subsequent encounters, will the claim reject?

At present, we do not know the answers to these questions. If we learn to code accurately in ICD-10-CM, we will never need to consider these possible problems.

Clinical Documentation Improvement (CDI) Impact on Coding: An Example

Since physician payments are based on the procedure code, the importance of the CPT code does not change with ICD-10-CM. However, diagnosis coding has not been critical in the past. We could use any reasonable code to allow payment. That is about to change. ICD-10-CM has codes based on laterality, severity, intent, and external causes. Payers will use this information to make certain they are paying claims appropriately. The addition of specific information in the medical record will allow coders to select the correct diagnosis code and hold off payer inquiries and avoid delayed payments.

Traditional documentation statement:

Mary Brown was treated for a painful small burn that she got this morning while making breakfast.

ICD-9-CM:	949.0—Burn, unspecified degree (there are 6.5 columns of burn codes) (ICD-9-CM note) "…extremely vague and should rarely be used."
ICD-10-CM:	T30.0—Burn of unspecified body region, unspecified degree (burn NOS) (Note: "Codes T20–T32 Burns and Corrosions are organized as burns by body site and degree.")
CPT:	99212 or 99213 or 16000—Initial treatment, first degree burn, when no more than local treatment is required

Better documentation statement:

Mary Brown was treated for a first degree painful small burn of the back of the left hand that she got this morning while making breakfast.

ICD-10-CM:	T23.162A—Burn of first degree of back of left hand (Note: Use additional code to identify the source, place, and intent of the burn.) (X00–X19, X75–X77, X96–X98, Y92). The external cause codes are not required by the federal government. State agencies and payers may require the external cause codes, but CMS does not require them for billing.

Correct documentation statement:

Mary Brown was treated for a painful small first degree burn at the back of the left hand that she got accidentally from the toaster this morning while making breakfast at home.

ICD-10-CM:	T23.162A	– and
	X15.1xxA	– Initial visit, contact with a hot toaster, and
	Y92.010	– Kitchen of a single family (private house) as the place of occurrence of the external cause.
	Y99.8	– Other external cause

Certain Infectious and Parasitic Diseases (A00–B99)

The ICD-10-CM begins with **Chapter 1** on infectious and parasitic diseases. While many of these are not seen in the typical physician's office, they may be very significant in the offices of other doctors. Occasionally, coders may be prompted to "use additional code" to identify an organism, such as B95.0 for Streptococcus, group A, as the cause of diseases classified elsewhere. This chapter has specific guideline instructions for coding HIV, antibiotic resistance, sepsis, septic shock, SIRS, and MRSA. When coding HIV, use the B20 code for symptomatic confirmed cases; asymptomatic status is Z21. Move carefully through this chapter.

This chapter contains the following blocks:

A00–A09	Intestinal infectious diseases
A15–A19	Tuberculosis
A20–A28	Certain zoonotic bacterial diseases
A30–A49	Other bacterial diseases
A50–A64	Infections with a predominately sexual mode of transmission
A65–A69	Other spirochetal diseases
A70–A74	Other diseases caused by chlamydiae
A75–A79	Rickettsioses
A80–A89	Viral and infections of the central nervous system
A90–A99	Arthropod-borne viral fevers and viral hemorrhagic fevers
B10	Other human herpes viruses
B15–B19	Viral hepatitis
B20	Human immunodeficiency virus [HIV] disease
B25–B34	Other viral diseases
B35–B49	Mycoses
B50–B64	Protozoal diseases
B65–B83	Helminthiasis
B85–B89	Pediculosis, acariasis, and other infestations
B90–B94	Sequelae of infectious and parasitic diseases
B95–B97	Bacterial and viral infectious agents
B99	Other infectious diseases

ICD-10-CM contains extensive official guidelines on coding HIV/AIDS and sepsis. There are additional instructions in each subcategory of codes advising "code first" or "use additional code." Code only what is stated or known in the medical record. If no additional information is provided in the worksheet, code only the specific term(s).

Name _____

Using the blocks on the previous page as guidance, locate the three-character categories for the following diagnoses:

Diagnoses	ICD-10-CM	ICD-9-CM
1. Amebic abscess of brain, liver, and lungs	_____	_____
2. Condyloma acuminatum	_____	_____
3. Tuberculous mononeuropathy	_____	_____
4. Cytomegaloviral hepatitis	_____	_____
5. Head-louse infestation	_____	_____
6. Viral meningitis	_____	_____
7. Swimmer's itch	_____	_____
8. Chronic viral hepatitis	_____	_____
9. Pinworm infection	_____	_____
10. Bone and joint tuberculosis	_____	_____

Name _____

Certain Infectious and Parasitic Diseases (A00–B99)

Using the alphabetic and tabular references, locate the following conditions and code to acceptable specificity, three to seven characters. Observe the coding instructions and include codes from other chapters as directed.

Diagnoses	ICD-10-CM	ICD-9-CM
1. Acute viral conjunctivitis from swimming pool	_____	_____
2. Illness from bite of rabid dog	_____	_____
3. Seven day fever	_____	_____
4. Cranial neuritis from Lyme disease	_____	_____
5. Ringworm	_____	_____
6. Trichomonal fluor	_____	_____
7. Syphilitic saddle nose	_____	_____
8. Echovirus intestinal infection	_____	_____
9. Dandy fever	_____	_____
10. Enterovirus D68	_____	_____
11. Group A shigellosis	_____	_____
12. Epstein-Barr viral mononucleosis with polyneuropathy	_____	_____
13. Gonorrheal condyloma of vulva	_____	_____
14. Subacute spongiform encephalopathy with dementia	_____	_____
15. Paratyphoid fever C	_____	_____
16. Rubella encephalitis	_____	_____
17. Urinary tract infection due to *E. coli*	_____	_____
18. Pulmonary paracoccidioidomycosis	_____	_____
19. Anaerobic sepsis	_____	_____
20. AIDS related complex	_____	_____
21. Early macular leprosy	_____	_____
22. Lupus vulgaris tuberculosis	_____	_____
23. Ebola viral fever	_____	_____
24. Colitis due to *Clostridium difficile*	_____	_____
25. Adenoviral meningitis	_____	_____

Neoplasms (C00–D49)

Chapter 2 begins with notes on (a) functional activity, (b) morphology [histology], (c) primary malignant neoplasms overlapping site boundaries, and (d) malignant neoplasm of ectopic tissue. Read these notes carefully and observe these instructions when coding from this chapter. An accurate code assignment begins with looking up the morphology (such as sarcoma, adenocarcinoma) in the Alphabetic Index of the classification system. The guidance provided in the Alphabetic Index will lead coders to the correct entry in the Neoplasm Table. Note that malignant neoplasms begin with C while benign and in situ neoplasms begin with a D. Observe the chapter-specific guidelines for neoplasms and sequencing rules for coding surgical treatment of malignant tumors, radiation, and chemotherapy.

This chapter contains the following blocks:

C00–C14	Malignant neoplasm of lip, oral cavity, and pharynx
C15–C26	Malignant neoplasm of digestive organs
C30–C39	Malignant neoplasm of respiratory and intrathoracic organs
C40–C41	Malignant neoplasm of bone and articular cartilage
C43–C44	Melanoma and other malignant neoplasms of skin
C45–C49	Malignant neoplasms of mesothelial and soft tissue
C50	Malignant neoplasm of breast
C51–C58	Malignant neoplasms of female genital organs
C60–C63	Malignant neoplasms of male genital organs
C64–C68	Malignant neoplasm of the urinary tract
C69–C72	Malignant neoplasms of the eye, brain, and other parts of the central nervous system
C73–C75	Malignant neoplasms of thyroid and other endocrine glands
C7A	Malignant neuroendocrine tumors
C7B	Secondary neuroendocrine tumors
C76–C80	Malignant neoplasms of ill-defined, other secondary and unspecified sites
C81–C96	Malignant neoplasms of lymphoid, hematopoietic, and related tissue
D00–D09	In situ neoplasms
D10–D36	Benign neoplasms, except benign neuroendocrine tumors
D3A	Benign neuroendocrine tumors
D37–D48	Neoplasms of uncertain behavior, polycythemia vera, and myelodysplastic syndrome
D49	Neoplasms of unspecified behavior

There are additional instructions within each block of codes advising "excludes 1" or "use additional code." Code only what is stated or known in the medical record. If no additional information is provided in the worksheet, code only the specific term(s).

Name _____

Using the blocks on the previous page as guidance, locate the three-character categories for the following diagnoses:

Diagnoses	ICD-10-CM	ICD-9-CM
1. Malignant tumor of tongue border	_____	_____
2. Benign heart neoplasm	_____	_____
3. Carcinoma in site anal margin	_____	_____
4. Acute myelomonocytic leukemia	_____	_____
5. Malignant neoplasm of pancreas tail	_____	_____
6. Kaposi's lung sarcoma	_____	_____
7. Breast carcinoma in situ	_____	_____
8. Benign frontal lobe tumor	_____	_____
9. Malignancy of left lung, lower lobe	_____	_____
10. Cancer of the bladder sphincter	_____	_____

Name _____

Neoplasms (C00–D49)

Using the alphabetic and tabular references, locate the following conditions and code to acceptable specificity, three to seven characters. Observe the coding instructions and include codes from other chapters as directed.

	Diagnoses	ICD-10-CM	ICD-9-CM
1.	Malignant carcinoma of right lower lobe of the lung	_____	_____
2.	Primary cancer of the cauda equina	_____	_____
3.	Cancer of the lower lip vermillion border	_____	_____
4.	Adenoma of thalamus, thalamus	_____	_____
5.	Metastatic carcinoma to the brain tumor	_____	_____
6.	Dermatofibroma, left abdominal wall	_____	_____
7.	Occipital lobe brain cancer	_____	_____
8.	Metastasis to nabothian gland	_____	_____
9.	Benign tumor of Cowper's gland	_____	_____
10.	Benign growth, left eyebrow	_____	_____
11.	Metastatic disease to the omentum	_____	_____
12.	Endometrial malignancy	_____	_____
13.	Benign neoplasm of the right renal pelvis	_____	_____
14.	Intramural uterine fibroid	_____	_____
15.	Cancer of the mesocolon	_____	_____
16.	Pancreatic duct cancer	_____	_____
17.	Lymphangiosarcoma of axilla	_____	_____
18.	Adenocarcinoma of right submaxillary gland	_____	_____
19.	In situ tracheal carcinoma	_____	_____
20.	Benign growth of the thymus	_____	_____
21.	Non-Hodgkins lymphoma, left axillary nodes	_____	_____
22.	Benign right breast tumor, 46-year-old male	_____	_____
23.	Cancer left lower lung lobe, 30+ years of tobacco use	_____	_____
24.	Retrobulbar malignancy, left eye	_____	_____
25.	Tonsil pillar carcinoma	_____	_____

Name _____

Diseases of the Blood and Blood-Forming Organs and Certain Disorders Involving the Immune Mechanism (D50–D89)

Chapter 3 begins with a note on the "excludes 2" in this chapter. Keep these exclusions in mind as you complete these worksheets. There are no chapter-specific coding guidelines for Chapter 3.

This chapter contains the following blocks:

D50–D53	Nutritional anemias
D55–D59	Hemolytic anemias
D60–D64	Aplastic and other anemias and other bone marrow failure syndromes
D65–D69	Coagulation defects, purpura, and other hemorrhagic conditions
D70–D77	Other disorders of blood and blood-forming organs
D78	Intraoperative and post procedural complication of the spleen
D80–D89	Certain disorders involving the immune mechanism

There are additional instructions within each block of codes advising "includes," "excludes 1," or "use additional code." Code only what is stated or known in the medical record. If no additional information is provided in the worksheet, code only the specific term(s).

Using the above blocks as guidance, locate the three-character categories for the following diagnoses:

	Diagnoses	ICD-10-CM	ICD-9-CM
1.	Christmas disease	_____	_____
2.	Cooley's anemia	_____	_____
3.	Infantile pseudoleukemia	_____	_____
4.	March hemoglobinuria	_____	_____
5.	Imerslund syndrome	_____	_____
6.	Aplastic anemia, NOS	_____	_____
7.	Hereditary leukomelanopathy	_____	_____
8.	Sideropenic dysphagia	_____	_____
9.	Emotional polycythemia	_____	_____
10.	Megakaryocytic hypoplasia	_____	_____

Name _____

Diseases of the Blood and Blood-Forming Organs and Certain Disorders Involving the Immune Mechanism (D50–D89)

Using the alphabetic and tabular references, locate the following conditions and code to acceptable specificity, three to seven characters. Observe the coding instructions and include codes from other chapters as directed.

Diagnoses	ICD-10-CM	ICD-9-CM
1. Antithromboplastinemia	_____	_____
2. Paroxysmal cold disease	_____	_____
3. Thrombocytopenia from extracorporeal blood circulation	_____	_____
4. Hypergammaglobulinemia	_____	_____
5. Megaloblastic anemia	_____	_____
6. Siderotic splenomegaly	_____	_____
7. Chronic hemoglobin Hb-SS disease with no documentation of crisis	_____	_____
8. Plummer-Vinson syndrome	_____	_____
9. Antineoplastic chemotherapy induced pancytopenia	_____	_____
10. Iron deficiency anemia	_____	_____
11. Mechanical hemolytic anemia	_____	_____
12. Vegan anemia	_____	_____
13. Von Willebrand's disease	_____	_____
14. Lazy leukocyte syndrome	_____	_____
15. Classical hemophilia	_____	_____
16. Intraoperative hemorrhage of spleen during surgery on the spleen	_____	_____
17. Splenitis	_____	_____
18. Stomatocytosis	_____	_____
19. Ideopathic allergic eosinophilia	_____	_____
20. Thrombocytopathy	_____	_____
21. Thalassemic variants	_____	_____
22. Blackfan-Diamond syndrome	_____	_____
23. Lymphocytopenia	_____	_____
24. Consumption coagulopathy	_____	_____
25. Goat's milk anemia	_____	_____

Name _____

Endocrine, Nutritional, and Metabolic Diseases (E00–E89)

Chapter 4 begins with notes stating all neoplasms are classified in Chapter 2; and codes E05.8, E07.0, E16–E31 and E34– may be used as additional codes. Also there is a general exclusion for transitory endocrine and metabolic disorders in a newborn. This chapter is where you find codes for Type 1 and Type 2 diabetes, thyroid problems, and obesity. There are many combination codes for diabetes and associated conditions such as nephropathy. Note that obesity is defined as a BMI of 30.0 and above. Be certain you review carefully the chapter-specific coding guidelines for Chapter 4.

This chapter contains the following blocks:

E00–E07	Disorders of thyroid gland
E08–E13	Diabetes mellitus
E15–E16	Other disorders of glucose regulation and pancreatic internal secretion
E20–E35	Disorders of other endocrine glands
E36	Intraoperative complications of endocrine system
E40–E46	Malnutrition
E50–E64	Other nutritional deficiencies
E65–E68	Overweight, obesity, and other hyperalimentation
E70–E88	Metabolic disorders
E89	Postprocedural endocrine and metabolic complications and disorders, not elsewhere classified

There are additional instructions within each block of codes advising "includes," "excludes 1," "excludes 2," "code also," or "use additional code." Only code what is documented in the health record. If no additional information is provided in the worksheet, code only the specific term(s). Note that intraoperative and postprocedural complications appear in separate blocks and are separately coded in this chapter.

Using the above blocks as guidance, locate the three-character categories for the following diagnoses:

	Diagnoses	ICD-10-CM	ICD-9-CM
1.	Type I diabetes	_____	_____
2.	Stein-Leventhal syndrome	_____	_____
3.	Simple nontoxic goiter	_____	_____
4.	Maple-syrup-urine disease	_____	_____
5.	Dysmetabolic syndrome X	_____	_____
6.	Familial hypercholesterolemia	_____	_____
7.	Postpancreatectomy diabetes mellitus	_____	_____
8.	Excess calorie morbid obesity	_____	_____
9.	Wermer's syndrome	_____	_____
10.	Hypoglycemia	_____	_____

Name _____

Endocrine, Nutritional, and Metabolic Diseases (E00–E89)

Using the alphabetic and tabular references, locate the following conditions and code to acceptable specificity, three to seven characters. Observe the coding instructions and include codes from other chapters as directed.

Diagnoses	ICD-10-CM	ICD-9-CM
1. Hashimoto's disease	_____	_____
2. Pseudohypoparathyroidism	_____	_____
3. Type 1 diabetes with diabetic cataract	_____	_____
4. Adrenal crisis	_____	_____
5. Night blindness from vitamin A deficiency	_____	_____
6. Graves' disease with thyrotoxic storm	_____	_____
7. Type 2 diabetes with Charcot's joints	_____	_____
8. Symptoms of early menopause	_____	_____
9. Group B hyperlipidemia	_____	_____
10. Type 1 diabetes mellitus with diabetic neuropathy	_____	_____
11. Elevated cholesterol and triglycerides	_____	_____
12. Uncontrolled Type II diabetes mellitus	_____	_____
13. Lactose intolerant	_____	_____
14. Type I diabetes with mild chronic kidney disease	_____	_____
15. Marasmic kwashiorkor	_____	_____
16. Diabetes insipidus	_____	_____
17. Type I diabetes, small superficial skin ulcer, left heel and midfoot	_____	_____
18. de Quervain syndrome	_____	_____
19. Delayed puberty	_____	_____
20. Calcium deficiency due to diet	_____	_____
21. X-linked adrenoleukodystrophy, age 15	_____	_____
22. Pickwickian syndrome	_____	_____
23. Pulmonary cystic fibrosis	_____	_____
24. Type 2 diabetes, nonproliferative retinopathy and macular edema	_____	_____
25. Hematoma of thyroid gland, developed during neck surgery	_____	_____

Name _____

Mental, Behavioral, and Neurodevelopmental Disorders (F01–F99)

Chapter 5 advises that psychological development disorders are included in this chapter. The "Excludes 2" instruction notes that symptoms, signs and abnormal clinical laboratory findings, not elsewhere classified, are R00–R99. There are codes here for use, abuse, and dependence on substances; schizophrenia, depression, bipolar I and II, anorexia, gambling, ADHD, and intellectual disabilities, sometimes called mental retardation, are included in this chapter. There are chapter-specific coding guidelines for pain and disorders due to psychoactive substance use.

This chapter contains the following blocks:

F01–F09	Mental disorders due to known physiological conditions
F10–F19	Mental and behavioral disorders due to psychoactive substance use
F20–F29	Schizophrenia, schizotypal, delusional, and other non-mood psychotic disorders
F30–F39	Mood [affective] disorders
F40–F48	Anxiety, dissociative, stress-related, somatoform, and other nonpsychotic mental disorders
F50–F59	Behavioral syndromes associated with physiological disturbances and physical factors
F60–F69	Disorders of adult personality and behavior
F70–F79	Intellectual disabilities
F80–F89	Pervasive and specific developmental disorders
F90–F98	Behavioral and emotional disorders with onset usually occurring in childhood and adolescence
F99	Unspecified mental disorder

There are additional instructions within each block of codes advising "includes," "Excludes 1," "Excludes 2," "code first," or "use additional code." Code only what is stated or known in the medical record. If no additional information is provided in the worksheet, code only the specific term(s).

Using the above blocks as guidance, locate the three-character categories for the following diagnoses:

	Diagnoses	**ICD-10-CM**	**ICD-9-CM**
1.	Nail-biting	_____	_____
2.	Aggressive personality disorder	_____	_____
3.	Depressive neurosis	_____	_____
4.	Intoxication from marijuana dependence	_____	_____
5.	Paranoia	_____	_____
6.	Dementia with combative behavior	_____	_____
7.	Frontal lobe syndrome	_____	_____
8.	Post-traumatic stress disorder	_____	_____
9.	Delirium from alcohol withdrawal	_____	_____
10.	Kleptomania	_____	_____

Name _____

Mental, Behavioral, and Neurodevelopmental Disorders (F01–F99)

Using the alphabetic and tabular references, locate the following conditions and code to acceptable specificity, three to seven characters. Observe the coding instructions and include codes from other chapters as directed.

Diagnoses	ICD-10-CM	ICD-9-CM
1. Opioid dependence	_____	_____
2. Episodic weekend glue sniffing abuse	_____	_____
3. Obsessive-compulsive personality	_____	_____
4. Frequent panic attacks	_____	_____
5. Asperger's disorder since age 4	_____	_____
6. Intoxication delirium from cannabis abuse	_____	_____
7. Post partum depression	_____	_____
8. Dysthymic personality disorder	_____	_____
9. Alcoholic intoxication	_____	_____
10. Acute infective psychosis	_____	_____
11. Exhibitionism	_____	_____
12. Undifferentiated chronic schizophrenia	_____	_____
13. Excessive fear of injections	_____	_____
14. IQ 27	_____	_____
15. PCP abuse with intoxication with perceptual disturbance	_____	_____
16. Stuttering, 4-year-old male	_____	_____
17. Hyperactive and inattentive attention-deficit disorder	_____	_____
18. Borderline schizophrenic	_____	_____
19. Childhood social anxiety	_____	_____
20. Anorexia nervosa	_____	_____
21. Adjustment reaction anxiety and depression	_____	_____
22. Bipolar, current episode manic without psychosis	_____	_____
23. Multiple personality disorder	_____	_____
24. Childhood pica disorder	_____	_____
25. Four-year-old girl with reactive attachment disorder	_____	_____

Name _____

Diseases of the Nervous System (G00–G99)

Chapter 6 begins with a list of "excludes 2" conditions that appear in other chapters. Observe these and other instructions for coding epilepsy (seizure disorders) and sequencing headaches and other pain symptoms. The chapter-specific coding guidelines provide instruction on dominant or nondominant side and the use of the pain codes in this chapter.

This chapter contains the following blocks:

G00–G09	Inflammatory diseases of the central nervous system
G10–G14	Systemic atrophies primarily affecting the central nervous system
G20–G26	Extrapyramidal and movement disorders
G30–G32	Other degenerative diseases of the nervous system
G35–G37	Demyelinating diseases of the central nervous system
G40–G47	Episodic and paroxysmal disorders
G50–G59	Nerve, nerve root and plexus disorders
G60–G65	Polyneuropathies and other disorders of the peripheral nervous system
G70–G73	Diseases of myoneural junction and muscle
G80–G83	Cerebral palsy and other paralytic syndromes
G89–G99	Other disorders of the nervous system

There are additional instructions within each block of codes advising "excludes 1," "excludes 2," "code first," "code also," or "use additional code." If no additional information is provided in the worksheet, code only the specific term(s).

Using the above blocks as guidance, locate the three-character categories for the following diagnoses:

Diagnoses	ICD-10-CM	ICD-9-CM
1. Pneumococcal meningitis	_____	_____
2. Communicating hydrocephalus	_____	_____
3. ALS	_____	_____
4. Periodic paralysis	_____	_____
5. Ideopathic nasal leak of cerebrospinal fluid	_____	_____
6. Necrotizing hemorrhagic encephalopathy, acute	_____	_____
7. Right carpal tunnel	_____	_____
8. Menstrual related hypersomnia	_____	_____
9. Parkinsonism	_____	_____
10. Guillian-Barre syndrome	_____	_____

Name _____

Diseases of the Nervous System (G00–G99)

Using the alphabetic and tabular references, locate the following conditions and code to acceptable specificity, three to seven characters. Observe the coding instructions and include codes from other chapters as directed.

Diagnoses	ICD-10-CM	ICD-9-CM
1. Tarsal tunnel syndrome, right	_____	_____
2. Huntington's chorea	_____	_____
3. Accidental lumbar puncture with cerebrospinal fluid leak	_____	_____
4. Premenstrual tension syndrome with intractable migraine	_____	_____
5. Dementia with lewy bodies	_____	_____
6. Hereditary Friedreich's ataxia	_____	_____
7. Narcolepsy and cataplexy, 15-year-old male	_____	_____
8. Tic douloureux	_____	_____
9. Pyogenic meningitis	_____	_____
10. Bilateral long-term upper diplegia	_____	_____
11. Acute motor neuropathy	_____	_____
12. Stiff-man syndrome	_____	_____
13. Neurogenic bladder from cauda equina	_____	_____
14. Duchenne muscular dystrophy	_____	_____
15. Early onset Alzheimer's	_____	_____
16. Multiple sclerosis	_____	_____
17. Myopathy from accidental methanol overdose last year	_____	_____
18. Torticollis, spasmodic type	_____	_____
19. Inflammatory demyelinating polyneuropathy, chronic	_____	_____
20. Chronic migraine, no aura, intractable, with status migrainosus	_____	_____
21. Meningitis, chronic	_____	_____
22. Reye's syndrome	_____	_____
23. Werdnig-Hoffman disease	_____	_____
24. Painful phantom limb syndrome	_____	_____
25. Chronic tension-type headache	_____	_____

Name _____

Diseases of the Eye and Adnexa (H00–H59)

Chapter 7 begins with a note to use an external cause code following the code for the eye condition, if applicable, to identify the cause of the eye condition. This is basically a "code also" instruction. Review carefully the extensive list of "excludes 2" conditions that may be the cause of the eye condition. Many of these are repeated in the individual blocks of codes. Note also that the glaucoma subcategory contains the first regular use of the "X" as a place holder to put the seventh character in the proper position. The chapter-specific guidelines provide direction on the use of the glaucoma codes.

This chapter contains the following blocks:

H00–H05	Disorders of the eyelid, lacrimal system, and orbit
H10–H11	Disorders of conjunctiva
H15–H22	Disorders of sclera, cornea, iris, and ciliary body
H25–H28	Disorders of lens
H30–H36	Disorders of choroid and retina
H40–H42	Glaucoma
H43–H44	Disorders of vitreous body and globe
H46–H47	Disorders of optic nerve and visual pathways
H49–H52	Disorders of ocular muscles, binocular movement, accommodation, and refraction
H53–H54	Visual disturbances and blindness
H55–H57	Other disorders of eye and adnexa
H59	Intraoperative and postprocedureal complications and disorders of eye and adnexa, not elsewhere classified

There are additional instructions within each block of codes advising "excludes 1," "excludes 2," "code first," "code also," or "use additional code." Code only what is stated or known in the medical record. If no additional information is provided in the worksheet, code only the specific term(s).

Using the above blocks as guidance, locate the three-character categories for the following diagnoses:

	Diagnoses	**ICD-10-CM**	**ICD-9-CM**
1.	Senile ectropion, right lower lid	_____	_____
2.	Poor drainage, right epiphora	_____	_____
3.	Abscess, right cornea	_____	_____
4.	Vitreous floaters	_____	_____
5.	Left age-related posterior subcapsular cataract	_____	_____
6.	Hemorrhage, right conjunctiva	_____	_____
7.	Left total retinal detachment	_____	_____
8.	Old-age macular degeneration	_____	_____
9.	Presbyopia	_____	_____
10.	Bilateral chronic conjunctivitis, uncomplicated	_____	_____

Name _____

Diseases of the Eye and Adnexa (H00–H59)

Using the alphabetic and tabular references, locate the following conditions and code to acceptable specificity, three to seven characters. Observe the coding instructions and include codes from other chapters as directed. Watch for the abbreviations FB (foreign body), OD (right eye), OS (left eye), and OU (both eyes).

Diagnoses	ICD-10-CM	ICD-9-CM
1. Bilateral irregular astigmatism	_____	_____
2. Stye, left lower lid	_____	_____
3. Prematurity retinopathy, stage 1, OU	_____	_____
4. Juvenile nuclear cataract, OS	_____	_____
5. Dermatitis (eczema) of left upper lid	_____	_____
6. Conjunctival pseudopterygium, OD	_____	_____
7. Moderate low-tension glaucoma, OS	_____	_____
8. Keratoconus, acute, unstable hydrops, OD	_____	_____
9. Pupillary margin degeneration, OS	_____	_____
10. Retinitis pigmentosa	_____	_____
11. Old metal FB, right lower lid	_____	_____
12. Scotoma, blindspot, OS	_____	_____
13. Bilateral retinopathy from the sun	_____	_____
14. Dry eye syndrome, OU	_____	_____
15. Open angle, low-tension, mild stage glaucoma, OS	_____	_____
16. Chronic allergic conjunctivitis, OU	_____	_____
17. Snow blindness, OU	_____	_____
18. Aphakia, OD	_____	_____
19. Retained FB (nail head), right anterior chamber	_____	_____
20. Old-age nuclear cataracts, OU	_____	_____
21. Right retinal central vein occlusion	_____	_____
22. Color-blindness	_____	_____
23. Dissociated nystagmus	_____	_____
24. Convergent strabismus, alternating A pattern	_____	_____
25. Left chorioretinal scarring from old retinal detachment surgery	_____	_____

Name _____

Diseases of the Ear and Mastoid Process (H60–H95)

Chapter 8 begins with a note to use the external cause code, if applicable, after the code for the ear condition to identify the cause of the ear condition. Review the "excludes 2" list on conditions that are coded in other chapters. There are no chapter-specific coding guidelines for Chapter 8.

This chapter contains the following blocks:

H60–H62	Diseases of the external ear
H65–H75	Diseases of the middle ear and mastoid
H80–H63	Diseases of the inner ear
H90–H94	Other disorders of the ear
H95	Intraoperative and postprocedural complications and disorders of the ear and mastoid process, not elsewhere classified

There are additional instructions within each block of codes advising "includes," "excludes 1," "excludes 2," "code first," or "use additional code." Code only what is stated or known in the medical record. If no additional information is provided in the worksheet, code only the specific term(s).

Using the above blocks as guidance, locate the three-character categories for the following diagnoses:

	Diagnoses	ICD-10-CM	ICD-9-CM
1.	Right attic cholesteatoma	_____	_____
2.	Boil, left external ear	_____	_____
3.	Bilateral Meniere's disease	_____	_____
4.	Otitis media, right	_____	_____
5.	Left chronic myringitis	_____	_____
6.	Left pinna perichondritis	_____	_____
7.	Bilateral presbycusis	_____	_____
8.	Tinnitus, right	_____	_____
9.	Mixed left hearing loss, normal right hearing	_____	_____
10.	Chronic mastoiditis	_____	_____

Name _____

Diseases of the Ear and Mastoid Process (H60–H95)

Using the alphabetic and tabular references, locate the following conditions and code to acceptable specificity, three to seven characters. Observe the coding instructions and include codes from other chapters as directed.

Diagnoses	ICD-10-CM	ICD-9-CM
1. Otalgia, right ear	_____	_____
2. Bilateral swimmer's ear	_____	_____
3. Sudden left idiopathic hearing loss	_____	_____
4. Bilateral sensorineural hearing loss	_____	_____
5. Right labyrinthine fistula	_____	_____
6. Bilateral chronic mastoiditis	_____	_____
7. Marginal tympanic membrane perforations, left	_____	_____
8. Left acoustic nerve disorder	_____	_____
9. Central positional nystagmus, left	_____	_____
10. Right bullous myringitis	_____	_____
11. Bony obstruction, right Eustachian tube	_____	_____
12. Right cochlear otosclerosis	_____	_____
13. Recurrent cholesteatoma in left postmastoidectomy cavity	_____	_____
14. Otitis externa with hemorrhage, left	_____	_____
15. Bilateral hearing loss from loud music	_____	_____
16. Chronic mucoid otitis media, left ear	_____	_____
17. Bilateral impacted cerumen	_____	_____
18. Right petrous bone inflammation	_____	_____
19. Labyrinthitis, left ear	_____	_____
20. Bilateral high frequency hearing loss	_____	_____
21. Right mastoid cholesteatoma	_____	_____
22. Total perforation, left tympanic membrane	_____	_____
23. Right middle ear polyp	_____	_____
24. Severe left Meniere's disease	_____	_____
25. Six-year-old with chronic bilateral serous otitis media, both parents are smokers	_____	_____

Name _____

Diseases of the Circulatory System (I00–I99)

Review the extensive "excludes 2" list on conditions that are coded in other chapters. **Chapter 9** codes will be used in many medical offices and some forms of the words can be confusing. Note that these codes begin with an "I," not the number "1." Move slowly through this chapter. Atherosclerosis is defined as the plaque buildup that occurs inside blood vessels. This chapter includes codes for hypertension, hypertensive heart disease with chronic kidney disease, angina, myocardial infarction (heart attack), and cerebrovascular disease. Specific chapter guidelines provide instruction on coding coronary heart disease (also called coronary artery disease) and other coronary and cerebrovascular conditions.

This chapter contains the following blocks:

I00–I02	Acute rheumatic fever
I05–I09	Chronic rheumatic heart diseases
I10–I15	Hypertensive diseases
I20–I25	Ischemic heart disease
I26–I28	Pulmonary heart disease and diseases of pulmonary circulation
I30–I15	Other forms of heart disease
I60–I69	Cerebrovascular diseases
I70–I79	Diseases of arteries, arterioles, and capillaries
I80–I89	Diseases of veins, lymphatic vessels, and lymph nodes, not elsewhere classified
I95–I99	Other and unspecified disorders of the circulatory system

There are additional instructions within each block of codes advising "includes," "excludes 1," "excludes 2," "code first," "code also," or "use additional code." Code only what is stated or known in the medical record. If no additional information is provided in the worksheet, code only the specific term(s).

Using the above blocks as guidance, locate the three-character categories for the following diagnoses:

Diagnoses	**ICD-10-CM**	**ICD-9-CM**
1. Postural hypotension	_____	_____
2. Buerger's disease	_____	_____
3. Acute diastolic heart disease	_____	_____
4. Chronic ischemic heart disease	_____	_____
5. Rheumatic mitral regurgitation	_____	_____
6. Mobitz II block	_____	_____
7. Left lower leg varicose veins with toe ulcer	_____	_____
8. High blood pressure	_____	_____
9. Subacute endocarditis	_____	_____
10. Unruptured cerebral aneurysm	_____	_____

Name _____

Diseases of the Circulatory System (I00–I99)

Using the alphabetic and tabular references, locate the following conditions and code to acceptable specificity, three to seven characters. Observe the coding instructions and include codes from other chapters as directed.

	Diagnoses	ICD-10-CM	ICD-9-CM
1.	Mitral valve insufficiency with aortic valve stenosis	_____	_____
2.	Sick sinus syndrome	_____	_____
3.	Hypertensive heart disease	_____	_____
4.	Dysphasia from cerebrovascular disease suffered last year	_____	_____
5.	Unstable angina	_____	_____
6.	Left ankle ulcer from leg atherosclerosis	_____	_____
7.	Thrombosis of left vertebral artery with infarction	_____	_____
8.	Congestive heart failure	_____	_____
9.	Healed myocardial infarction	_____	_____
10.	Left vertebral artery stenosis and occlusion	_____	_____
11.	Unruptured abdominal aortic aneurysm	_____	_____
12.	Scrotal varices	_____	_____
13.	Postmastectomy elephantiasis	_____	_____
14.	Atherosclerosis of bypassed graft (autologous saphenous vein) with unstable angina	_____	_____
15.	Thrombophlebitis and phlebitis, left femoral vein	_____	_____
16.	Bilateral varicose leg veins, asymptomatic	_____	_____
17.	Alcohol dependence with alcoholic cardiomyopathy	_____	_____
18.	Cardiorenal hypertension, stage 2 kidney disease	_____	_____
19.	Intermittent claudication	_____	_____
20.	Idiopathic gangrene	_____	_____
21.	STEMI of left anterior descending coronary artery	_____	_____
22.	Varicose veins, left leg, with inflammation	_____	_____
23.	Raynaud's disease	_____	_____
24.	Pulmonary hypertension	_____	_____
25.	Chronic atrial fibrillation	_____	_____

Name _____

Diseases of the Respiratory System (J00–J99)

Chapter 10 begins with a note: When a respiratory condition is described as occurring in more than one site and is not specifically indexed, it should be classified to the lower anatomic site (e.g. tracheobronchitis to bronchitis in J40). The terms acute, chronic, and acute exacerbation of a chronic disorder, and other conditions could change the coding order. Observe the chapter-specific coding guidelines for COPD, asthma, influenza, and pneumonia.

This chapter contains the following blocks:

J00–J06	Acute upper respiratory infections
J09–J18	Influenza and pneumonia
J20–J22	Other acute lower respiratory infections
J30–J39	Other diseases of the upper respiratory tract
J40–J47	Chronic lower respiratory diseases
J60–J70	Lung diseases due to external agents
J80–J84	Other respiratory diseases principally affecting the interstitium
J85–J86	Suppurative and necrotic conditions of the lower respiratory tract
J90–J94	Other diseases of the pleura
J95	Intraoperative and postprocedural complications and disorders of respiratory system, not elsewhere classified
J96–J99	Other diseases of the respiratory system

There are additional instructions within each block of codes advising, "includes," "Excludes 1," "Excludes 2," "code first," "code also," or "use additional code." Code only what is stated or known in the medical record. If no additional information is provided in the worksheet, code only the specific term(s).

Using the above blocks as guidance, locate the three-character categories for the following diagnoses:

Diagnoses	ICD-10-CM	ICD-9-CM
1. Pulmonary edema	_____	_____
2. Mild intermittent asthma	_____	_____
3. Common cold	_____	_____
4. Mendelson's syndrome	_____	_____
5. Acute chemical bronchitis	_____	_____
6. Influenza	_____	_____
7. Quinsy	_____	_____
8. Black lung disease	_____	_____
9. Acute rhinovirus bronchitis	_____	_____
10. Severe acute respiratory syndrome	_____	_____

Name _____

Diseases of the Respiratory System (J00–J99)

Using the alphabetic and tabular references, locate the following conditions and code to acceptable specificity, three to seven characters. Observe the coding instructions and include codes from other chapters as directed.

	Diagnoses	ICD-10-CM	ICD-9-CM
1.	Pollen induced allergic rhinitis	_____	_____
2.	Acute sinus infection	_____	_____
3.	Chronic tonsillitis	_____	_____
4.	Mediastinal emphysema	_____	_____
5.	Laryngeal edema	_____	_____
6.	Silicosis	_____	_____
7.	A/H5N1 Influenza with pneumonia	_____	_____
8.	Moderately persistent asthma with status asthamaticus	_____	_____
9.	Pulmonary fibrosis, idiopathic	_____	_____
10.	Return visit for lung fibrosis from radon exposure	_____	_____
11.	Chronic bronchitis	_____	_____
12.	E. coli bronchopneumonia	_____	_____
13.	Hypoxia with chronic respiratory failure	_____	_____
14.	COPD	_____	_____
15.	Acute spontaneous pneumothorax	_____	_____
16.	Pulmonary interstitial glycogenosis	_____	_____
17.	Respiratory trouble from smoke inhalation	_____	_____
18.	Frontal sinus infection	_____	_____
19.	Aspiration pneumonia	_____	_____
20	Pleural effusion	_____	_____
21.	Laryngotracheitis	_____	_____
22.	Right maxillary sinus polyp	_____	_____
23.	Methacillin resistant Staphylococcus aureus pneumonia	_____	_____
24.	Acute bronchiolitis	_____	_____
25.	Pulmonary emphysema	_____	_____

Name _____

Diseases of the Digestive System (K00–K95)

There are no chapter-specific coding guidelines for **Chapter 11**. There is an extensive list of "Excludes 2" conditions that appear in other chapters. Review and observe these exclusions when coding digestive disorders including hernias and noninfective enteritis and colitis, including Crohn's disease.

This chapter contains the following blocks:

K00–K14	Diseases of oral cavity and salivary glands
K20–K31	Diseases of esophagus, stomach, and duodenum
K35–K39	Diseases of appendix
K40–K46	Hernia
K50–K52	Noninfective enteritis and colitis
K55–K64	Other diseases of intestines
K65–K68	Diseases of peritoneum and retroperitoneum
K70–K77	Diseases of liver
K80–K87	Disorders of gallbladder, biliary tract, and pancreas
K90–K95	Other diseases of the digestive system

There are additional instructions within each block of codes advising "includes," "excludes 1," "excludes 2," "code first," "use additional code," or "code also." Code only what is stated or known in the medical record. If no additional information is provided in the worksheet, code only the specific term(s).

Using the above blocks as guidance, locate the three-character categories for the following diagnoses:

	Diagnoses	ICD-10-CM	ICD-9-CM
1.	Right inguinal hernia	_____	_____
2.	Mesenteric lipodystrophy	_____	_____
3.	Cirrhosis of the liver	_____	_____
4.	Microdontia	_____	_____
5.	Gastric band infection	_____	_____
6.	Acute appendicitis	_____	_____
7.	Regional colitis	_____	_____
8.	Hemorrhagic angiodysplasia of the colon	_____	_____
9.	Gallbladder gangrene	_____	_____
10.	Esophageal erosion	_____	_____

Name _____

Diseases of the Digestive System (K00–K95)

Using the alphabetic and tabular references, locate the following conditions and code to acceptable specificity, three to seven characters. Observe the coding instructions and include codes from other chapters as directed.

Diagnoses	ICD-10-CM	ICD-9-CM
1. Stenosis of salivary duct, left	_____	_____
2. Ruptured appendix with peritonitis	_____	_____
3. Irritable bowel syndrome	_____	_____
4. Chronic hemorrhage from a gastric ulcer	_____	_____
5. Impacted left lower wisdom tooth	_____	_____
6. Crohn's disease with fistula	_____	_____
7. Strangulated midline ventral hernia	_____	_____
8. Chronic gastritis	_____	_____
9. Perianal abscess	_____	_____
10. Nonalcoholic fatty liver disease	_____	_____
11. Significant aphthous stomatitis	_____	_____
12. Celiac disease	_____	_____
13. Post-op dumping syndrome	_____	_____
14. Chronic appendicitis	_____	_____
15. Liver disorder caused by schistosomiasis	_____	_____
16. Sialoadenitis, acute	_____	_____
17. Chronic cholecystis with obstruction and bile duct stone	_____	_____
18. Post-op pelvic adhesions, 46-year-old male	_____	_____
19. Chronic duodenal ulcer	_____	_____
20. Diverticulosis of large and small intestine	_____	_____
21. Colon polyp	_____	_____
22. Obstructed incarcerated umbilical hernia	_____	_____
23. Chronic gingivitis from plaque	_____	_____
24. Acute pancreatitis	_____	_____
25. Recurrent gastroenteritis and colitis following suicide attempt (methanol) 12 years ago	_____	_____

Name _____

Diseases of the Skin and Subcutaneous Tissue (L00–L99)

Chapter 12 begins with an extensive list of "excludes 2" conditions that appear in other chapters. There are chapter-specific coding guidelines for documenting and coding the staging of pressure ulcers.

This chapter contains the following blocks:

L00–L08	Infections of the skin and subcutaneous tissue
L10–L14	Bullous disorders
L20–L30	Dermatitis and eczema
L40–L45	Papulosquamous disorders
L49–L54	Urticaria and erythema
L55–L59	Radiation-related disorders of the skin and subcutaneous tissue
L6O–L75	Disorders of skin appendages
L76	Intraoperative and postprocedural complications of skin and subcutaneous tissue
L80–L99	Other disorders of the skin and subcutaneous tissue

There are additional instructions within each block of codes advising "includes," "excludes 1," "excludes 2," "code first," "use additional code," or "code also." Code only what is stated or known in the medical record. If no additional information is provided in the worksheet, code only the specific term(s).

Using the above blocks as guidance, locate the three-character categories for the following diagnoses:

		ICD-10-CM	ICD-9-CM
1.	Duhring's disease	_____	_____
2.	Psoriatic arthritis mutilans	_____	_____
3.	Boil on the left scapula	_____	_____
4.	Nonbullous erythema multiformae	_____	_____
5.	Hyperhydrosis	_____	_____
6.	Allergic dermatitis from face cream	_____	_____
7.	Cradle cap	_____	_____
8.	Corn on left great toe	_____	_____
9.	Pilonidal abscess	_____	_____
10.	Senile keratosis	_____	_____

Name _____

Diseases of the Skin and Subcutaneous Tissue (L00–L99)

Using the alphabetic and tabular references, locate the following conditions and code to acceptable specificity, three to seven characters. Observe the coding instructions and include codes from other chapters as directed.

Diagnoses	ICD-10-CM	ICD-9-CM
1. Lupus erythematosus	_____	_____
2. Ingrown right great toenail	_____	_____
3. Puncture of skin while treating dermatitis, accidental	_____	_____
4. Right forearm cellulitis	_____	_____
5. Bullous impetigo	_____	_____
6. Stage 2 healing pressure ulcer, right elbow	_____	_____
7. Chronic urticaria	_____	_____
8. Senear-Usher syndrome	_____	_____
9. Puritus ani	_____	_____
10. Diaper rash	_____	_____
11. Acne vulgaris	_____	_____
12. Pityriasis rosea	_____	_____
13. Stage 2 healing pressure ulcer, right hip	_____	_____
14. Eczema	_____	_____
15. Boil, left buttock	_____	_____
16. Second degree sunburn of the back	_____	_____
17. Irritation dermatitis from contact with nickel in ring	_____	_____
18. Folliculitis, left cheek	_____	_____
19. Dermatitis from the sun	_____	_____
20. Keloid scar, lower left abdomen	_____	_____
21. Sebaceous cyst of the neck	_____	_____
22. Contact dermatitis from allergy to dog hair	_____	_____
23. Alopecia universalis	_____	_____
24. Rhinophyma	_____	_____
25. Chronic venous hypertension with right calf ulcer exposing muscle necrosis	_____	_____

Name _____

Diseases of the Musculoskeletal System and Connective Tissue (M00–M99)

Chapter 13 begins with a note to use the external cause code following the musculoskeletal condition code, if applicable; and an extensive list of "excludes 2" conditions that appear in other chapters.

Review and observe these exclusions when coding musculoskeletal and connective tissue disorders.

This chapter contains the following blocks:

M00–M02	Infectious arthropathies
M05–M14	Inflammatory polyarthropathies
M15–M19	Osteoarthritis
M20–M25	Other joint disorders
M26–M27	Dentofacial anomalies (including malocclusion) and other disorders of jaw
M30–M36	Systemic connective tissue disorders
M40–M43	Deforming dorsopathies
M45–M49	Spondylopathies
M50–M54	Other dorsopathies
M60–M63	Disorders of muscles
M65–M67	Disorders of synovium and tendon
M70–M79	Other soft tissue disorders
M80–M85	Disorders of bone density and structure
M86–M90	Other osteopathies
M91–M94	Chondropathies
M95	Other disorders of the musculoskeletal system and connective tissue
M96	Intraoperative and postprocedural complications and disorders of musculoskeletal system, not elsewhere classified
M99	Biomechanical lesions, not elsewhere classified

There are additional instructions within each block of codes advising "includes," "Excludes 1," "Excludes 2" "code first," "use additional code," or "code also." Code only what is stated or known in the medical record. If no additional information is provided in the worksheet, code only the specific term(s).

Name _____

Using the blocks on the previous page as guidance, locate the three-character categories for the following diagnoses:

Diagnoses	ICD-10-CM	ICD-9-CM
1. Acute gout	_____	_____
2. Osteoarthritis, right knee, following a fall	_____	_____
3. Calcium in the bursa, left ankle	_____	_____
4. Legg-Calve-Perthes, right leg	_____	_____
5. Effusion, left elbow	_____	_____
6. Right foot rheumatoid arthritis nodule	_____	_____
7. Left tennis elbow	_____	_____
8. Lumbar kissing spine	_____	_____
9. Single bone cyst, right humerus	_____	_____
10. Left lumbago and sciatica	_____	_____

Name _____

Diseases of the Musculoskeletal System and Connective Tissue (M00–M99)

Using the alphabetic and tabular references, locate the following conditions and code to acceptable specificity, three to seven characters. Observe the coding instructions and include codes from other chapters as directed.

	Diagnoses	ICD-10-CM	ICD-9-CM
1.	Short Achilles tendon, right ankle	_____	_____
2.	Chronic gout, right big toe, cause unknown	_____	_____
3.	Recurrent left knee dislocation	_____	_____
4.	Lumbosacral scoliosis from cerebral palsy	_____	_____
5.	Low back pain	_____	_____
6.	Pneumococcal arthritis, right wrist	_____	_____
7.	Dry socket left lower jaw	_____	_____
8.	Trigger finger, right middle finger	_____	_____
9.	Left wrist ganglion	_____	_____
10.	Spontaneous rupture of extensor tendon, right forearm	_____	_____
11.	Systemic lupus erythematosus	_____	_____
12.	Cervical vertebral osteomyelitis	_____	_____
13.	Arthropathy, left elbow, following gastric bypass	_____	_____
14.	Initial encounter for stress fracture, thoracic vertebra	_____	_____
15.	Partial tear of left rotator cuff	_____	_____
16.	Rupture of right wrist synovium	_____	_____
17.	Flat feet, not congenital	_____	_____
18.	Fibromyalgia	_____	_____
19.	Bursitis, right knee	_____	_____
20.	Rheumatoid arthritis with myopathy, right hand	_____	_____
21.	Subsequent visit for a healing, collapsed cervical vertebral fracture	_____	_____
22.	Radiculopathy L5-S1	_____	_____
23.	Recurrent muscle spasms, left calf	_____	_____
24.	Postlaminectomy kyphosis	_____	_____
25.	ER visit for old-age osteoporosis and pathological fracture of right hip	_____	_____

Name _____

Diseases of the Genitourinary System (N00–N99)

Chapter 14 begins with an extensive list of "excludes 2" conditions that appear in other chapters. Review and observe these exclusions when coding genitourinary disorders.

This chapter contains the following blocks:

N00–N08	Glomerular diseases
N10–N19	Renal tubulo-interstitial diseases
N17–N19	Acute kidney failure and chronic kidney disease
N20–N23	Urolithiasis
N25–N29	Other disorders of kidney and ureter
N30–N39	Other diseases of the urinary system
N40–N53	Diseases of male genital organs
N60–N65	Disorders of breast
N70–N77	Inflammatory diseases of female pelvis organs
N80–N98	Noninflammatory disorders of female genital tract
N99	Intraoperative and posprocedural complications and disorders of genitourinary system, not elsewhere classified

There are additional instructions within each block of codes advising "Includes," "Excludes 1," "Excludes 2," "code first," "use additional code," or "code also." Code only what is stated or known in the medical record. If no additional information is provided in the worksheet, code only the specific term(s).

Using the above blocks as guidance, locate the three-character categories for the following diagnoses:

Diagnoses	ICD-10-CM	ICD-9-CM
1. Overactive bladder	_____	_____
2. Acute prostatitis	_____	_____
3. Fibrocystic breast disease	_____	_____
4. Infertility from tubal stenosis	_____	_____
5. Glomerulonephritis	_____	_____
6. Kidney stone	_____	_____
7. Bertholin's gland cyst	_____	_____
8. Testicular atrophy	_____	_____
9. Paraphimosis	_____	_____
10. Metrorrhagia	_____	_____

Name _____

Diseases of the Genitourinary System (N00–N99)

Using the alphabetic and tabular references, locate the following conditions and code to acceptable specificity, three to seven characters. Observe the coding instructions and include codes from other chapters as directed.

Diagnoses	ICD-10-CM	ICD-9-CM
1. Stage 2 chronic kidney disease	_____	_____
2. Asymptomatic enlarged prostate	_____	_____
3. Chronic salpingo-oophoritis	_____	_____
4. Paravaginal cystocele	_____	_____
5. Breast lump	_____	_____
6. Nocturnal enuresis	_____	_____
7. Cystostomy stoma malfunction	_____	_____
8. Acute cystitis, no hematuria	_____	_____
9. Stress incontinence, 54-year-old male	_____	_____
10. Encysted hydrocele	_____	_____
11 Uterine endometriosis	_____	_____
12. Nephroptosis	_____	_____
13. Posthysterectomy vaginal vault prolapsed	_____	_____
14. Urethral stricture from injury, 42-year-old male	_____	_____
15. Acute glomerulonephritis	_____	_____
16. Chronic uremia	_____	_____
17. Hydronephrosis	_____	_____
18. Misshaped left breast following reconstruction	_____	_____
19. Primary amenorrhea	_____	_____
20. Pelvic inflammatory disease	_____	_____
21. Painful erection	_____	_____
22. Mittelschmerz	_____	_____
23. Ovarian hyperstimulation from induced ovulation	_____	_____
24. Senile atrophic vaginitis	_____	_____
25. Male infertility	_____	_____

Name _____

Pregnancy, Childbirth, and the Puerperium (O00-O9A)

Chapter 15 begins with notes that (1) these codes are only used on maternal records, and (2) trimesters are counted from the first day after the last menstrual period. There is a note that pregnancy requires a code from category Z3A to identify the specific week of pregnancy. Review also the "Excludes 1" and "Excludes 2" notes. There is a significant change in the classification system between ICD-9-CM and ICD-10-CM. The 5th digit subclassification in ICD-9-CM has been deleted. One of the key axis features in ICD-10-CM is identification of the trimester. Guidelines allow for consistency of reporting trimester. In addition, codes Z3A captures the exact weeks of gestation.

This chapter contains the following blocks:

O00-O08	Pregnancy with abortive outcome
O09	Supervision of high-risk pregnancy
O10–O16	Edema, proteinuria and hypertensive disorders in pregnancy, childbirth and the puerperium
020–O29	Other maternal disorders predominantly related to pregnancy
O30–O48	Maternal care related to the fetus and amniotic cavity and possible delivery problems
O60–O77	Complications of labor and delivery
O80–O82	Encounter for delivery
O85–092	Complications predominantly related to the puerperium
O94–O9A	Other obstetric conditions not elsewhere classified

There are additional instructions within each block of codes advising "includes," "Excludes 1," "Excludes 2," "code first," "code also," or use additional code." Code only what is stated or known in the medical record. If no additional information is provided in the worksheet, code only the specific term(s).

Using the above blocks as guidance, locate the three-character categories for the following diagnoses:

Diagnoses	ICD-10-CM	ICD-9-CM
1. Fallopian pregnancy	_____	_____
2. Mild hyperemesis gravidarum, 17 weeks	_____	_____
3. Spontaneous miscarriage	_____	_____
4. Abnormal prenatal chromosome lab test	_____	_____
5. Bladder infection of pregnancy	_____	_____
6. Braxton Hicks contractions	_____	_____
7. Prenatal deep-vein thrombosis	_____	_____
8. Shock following induced abortion	_____	_____
9. Pregnancy complicated by physical abuse, 16-year-old	_____	_____
10. Gestational diabetes mellitus	_____	_____

Name _____

Pregnancy, Childbirth, and the Puerperium (O00–O9A)

Using the alphabetic and tabular references, locate the following conditions and code to acceptable specificity, three to seven characters. Observe the coding instructions and include codes from other chapters as directed.

Diagnoses	ICD-10-CM	ICD-9-CM
1. Uterine rupture during labor	_____	_____
2. Delivery of triplets by Cesarean Section, all liveborn (delivery at 37 weeks)	_____	_____
3. Excessive weight gain, 29 weeks	_____	_____
4. Placenta previa with hemorrhage, 19 weeks	_____	_____
5. Partial hydatidiform mole	_____	_____
6. Triplet pregnancy, 24 weeks	_____	_____
7. Manage high-risk pregnancy, first trimester (previous stillborn)	_____	_____
8. Failed termination of pregnancy with hemorrhage	_____	_____
9. Acute kidney failure after spontaneous abortion	_____	_____
10. Normal pregnancy, delivery of live male infant	_____	_____
11. Cracked nipple from lactation	_____	_____
12. Pregnant female at 15 weeks seen for spotting	_____	_____
13. Preterm labor, delivery of female infant at term, 30 weeks	_____	_____
14. Husband's psychological abuse complicates 25 week pregnancy	_____	_____
15. Uremia following ectopic pregnancy	_____	_____
16. Two-pack a day cigarette use, complicating pregnancy	_____	_____
17. Renal shutdown following induced termination	_____	_____
18. Age 15, supervision of third pregnancy, 17 weeks	_____	_____
19. Precipitate labor, undelivered	_____	_____
20. Cardiomyopathy developed in third trimester	_____	_____
21. Cord entanglement making labor and delivery difficult	_____	_____
22. Hemorrhoids of pregnancy, 15 weeks	_____	_____
23. Postpartum hemorrhoids	_____	_____
24. Normal OB care, first trimester	_____	_____
25. Missed abortion, 16 weeks	_____	_____

Name _____

Certain Conditions Originating in the Perinatal Period (P00–P96)

Chapter 16 begins with a note that these codes are used only on newborn records, never on maternal records. There is an "includes" note defining conditions that originate in the fetal or perinatal period (through the first 28 days after birth even if the morbidity occurs later). Review the extensive list of "Excludes 2" conditions that appear in other chapters. Review and observe these directions when coding this chapter.

This chapter contains the following blocks:

P00–P04	Newborn affected by maternal factors and by complications of pregnancy, labor, and delivery
P05–P08	Disorder of newborn related to length of gestation and fetal growth
P09	Abnormal findings on neonatal screening
P10–P15	Birth trauma
P19–P29	Respiratory and cardiovascular disorders specific to the perinatal period
P35–P39	Infections specific to the perinatal period
P50–P61	Hemorrhagic and hematological disorders of newborn
P70–P74	Transitory endocrine and metabolic disorders specific to newborn
P76–P78	Digestive system disorders of newborn
P80–P83	Conditions involving the integument and temperature regulation of newborn
P84	Other problems with newborn
P90–P96	Other disorders originating in the perinatal period

There are additional instructions within each block of codes advising "includes," "Excludes 1," "Excludes 2," "code first," "code also," or "use additional code." Code only what is stated or known in the medical record. If no additional information is provided in the worksheet, code only the specific term(s).

Name _____

Using the blocks on the previous page as guidance, locate the three-character categories for the following diagnoses:

Diagnoses	ICD-10-CM	ICD-9-CM
1. Crack baby	_____	_____
2. Newborn possibly affected by amniocentesis	_____	_____
3. Wet lung syndrome	_____	_____
4. Polycythemia neonatorum	_____	_____
5. Localized subdural hematoma from birth injury	_____	_____
6. Failure to thrive in 14-day-old male	_____	_____
7. Prematurity hyperbilirubinemia	_____	_____
8. Pneumonia secondary to aspiration of blood	_____	_____
9. Newborn weighing 10.2 lbs.	_____	_____
10. Fetal chignon from vacuum extractor	_____	_____

Current Procedural Terminology ©2014 American Medical Association. All Rights Reserved.

Name _____

Certain Conditions Originating in the Perinatal Period (P00–P96)

Using the alphabetic and tabular references, locate the following conditions and code to acceptable specificity, three to seven characters. Observe the coding instructions and include codes from other chapters as directed.

	Diagnoses	ICD-10-CM	ICD-9-CM
1.	Maternal death suspected to affect newborn	_____	_____
2.	Meconium aspiration pneumonia	_____	_____
3.	Small-for-dates newborn, 2,200 grams	_____	_____
4.	Newborn vitamin K deficiency	_____	_____
5.	Congenital rubella pneumonitis		
6.	Infant-of-a-diabetic-mother syndrome		
7.	Congenital pneumonia due to *E. coli*	_____	_____
8.	Cesarian delivery perhaps affecting newborn	_____	_____
9.	Newborn *Staphylococcus aureus* sepsis	_____	_____
10.	Possible impact on newborn from tight cord around neck	_____	_____
11.	Post-term newborn, 41 weeks	_____	_____
12.	Newborn 32 weeks, weighting 1,300 grams	_____	_____
13.	Neonatal bruising with jaundice	_____	_____
14.	Obstructive newborn apnea	_____	_____
15.	Newborn regurgitation/rumination	_____	_____
16.	Bradycardia in newborn	_____	_____
17.	Grey baby syndrome	_____	_____
18.	Meconiun ileus	_____	_____
19.	Perinatal pneumothorax	_____	_____
20.	Congenital toxoplasmosis	_____	_____
21.	Mother is cocaine dependent, newborn has withdrawal symptoms	_____	_____
22.	Facial palsy from birth injury	_____	_____
23.	Wilson-Mikity syndrome	_____	_____
24.	Newborn may be affected by abruptio placenta	_____	_____
25.	Newborn hypoxia	_____	_____

Name _____

Congenital Malformations, Deformations, and Chromosomal Abnormalities (Q00–Q99)

Chapter 17 begins with a note that codes from this chapter are not used on maternal or fetal records. There is an "excludes 2" reference to inborn errors of metabolism. Review and observe these notes and exclusions when coding this chapter.

This chapter contains the following blocks:

Q00–Q07	Congenital malformations of the nervous system
Q10–Q18	Congenital malformations of eye, ear, face, and neck
Q20–Q28	Congenital malformations of the circulatory system
Q30–Q34	Congenital malformations of the respiratory system
Q35–Q37	Cleft lip and cleft palate
Q38–Q45	Other congenital malformations of the digestive system
Q50–Q56	Congenital malformations of genital organs
Q60–Q64	Congenital malformations of the urinary system
Q65–Q79	Congenital malformations and deformations of the musculoskeletal system
Q80–Q89	Other congenital malformations
Q90–Q99	Chromosomal abnormalities, not elsewhere classified

There are additional instructions within each block of codes advising "includes," "Excludes 1," "Excludes 2," "code first," "code also," or "use additional code." Code only what is stated or known in the medical record. If no additional information is provided in the worksheet, code only the specific term(s).

Using the above blocks as guidance, locate the three-character categories for the following diagnoses:

	Diagnoses	ICD-10-CM	ICD-9-CM
1.	Congenital absence of the outer ear	_____	_____
2.	Congenital partial dislocation of left hip	_____	_____
3.	Dandy-Walker syndrome	_____	_____
4.	Tetralogy of Fallot	_____	_____
5.	Ankyloglossia	_____	_____
6.	Bicornate uterus	_____	_____
7.	Harelip	_____	_____
8.	Supernumerary ear	_____	_____
9.	Strawberry nevus	_____	_____
10.	Polydactyly	_____	_____

Name _____

Congenital Malformations, Deformations, and Chromosomal Abnormalities (Q00–Q99)

Using the alphabetic and tabular references, locate the following conditions and code to acceptable specificity, three to seven characters. Observe the coding instructions and include codes from other chapters as directed.

	Diagnoses	ICD-10-CM	ICD-9-CM
1.	Fragile X syndrome	_____	_____
2.	Congenital aortic insufficiency	_____	_____
3.	Penile hypospadias	_____	_____
4.	Stenosis of aqueduct of Sylvius	_____	_____
5.	Bilateral webbed toes	_____	_____
6.	Harlequin fetus	_____	_____
7.	Hereditary cystic lung disease	_____	_____
8.	Trisomy 21, IQ 40–50	_____	_____
9.	Acrocephaly	_____	_____
10.	Cleft soft palate and bilateral cleft lip	_____	_____
11.	Lumbosacral spina bifida, no hydrocephalus	_____	_____
12.	Congenital absence of both lower limbs	_____	_____
13.	Arnold-Chiari syndrome and spina bifida	_____	_____
14.	Congenital AV aneurysm pulmonary artery	_____	_____
15.	Spina bifida occulta	_____	_____
16.	Congenital right cataract	_____	_____
17.	Vrolik's disease	_____	_____
18.	Autosomal recessive polycystic kidney disease	_____	_____
19.	Microgastria	_____	_____
20.	Patent ductus arteriosus	_____	_____
21.	Congenital pancreatic agenesis	_____	_____
22.	Congenital talipes equinovarus	_____	_____
23	Sponge kidney	_____	_____
24.	Dextrocardia	_____	_____
25.	Prune-belly syndrome	_____	_____

Name _____

Symptoms, Signs, and Abnormal Clinical and Laboratory Findings, Not Elsewhere Classified (R00–R99)

Chapter 18 begins with long note on the uses of these codes and a list of "excludes 2" conditions that appear in other chapters. Review and observe all notes and exclusions when coding this chapter.

This chapter contains the following blocks:

R00–R09	Symptoms and signs involving the circulatory and respiratory systems
R10–R19	Symptoms and signs involving the digestive system and abdomen
R20–R23	Symptoms and signs involving the skin and subcutaneous tissue
R25–R29	Symptoms and signs involving the nervous and musculoskeletal systems
R30–R39	Symptoms and signs involving the genitourinary system
R40–R46	Symptoms and signs involving cognition, perceptions, emotional state, and behavior
R47–R49	Symptoms and signs involving speech and voice
R50–R69	General symptoms and signs
R70–R77	Abnormal findings on examination of blood without diagnosis
R80–R82	Abnormal finding on examination of urine without diagnosis
R83–R89	Abnormal findings on examination of other body fluids, substances, and tissues without diagnosis
R90–R94	Abnormal findings on diagnostic imaging and in function studies without diagnosis
R97	Abnormal tumor markers
R99	Ill-defined and unknown cause of mortality

There are additional instructions within each block of codes advising "includes," "excludes 1," "excludes 2," "code first," "code also," or "use additional code." Code only what is stated or known in the medical record. If no additional information is provided in the worksheet, code only the specific term(s).

Name _____

Using the blocks on the previous page as guidance, locate the three-character categories for the following diagnoses:

Diagnoses	ICD-10-CM	ICD-9-CM
1. Slow heart beat	_____	_____
2. Hoarseness	_____	_____
3. Cheyne-Stokes respiration	_____	_____
4. Elevated fasting glucose	_____	_____
5. Bilious emesis	_____	_____
6. Anterior chest-wall pain	_____	_____
7. Memory loss	_____	_____
8. Occult blood in stools	_____	_____
9. Lymphadenopathy	_____	_____
10. Anhedonia	_____	_____

Name _____

Symptoms, Signs, and Abnormal Clinical and Laboratory Findings, Not Elsewhere Classified (R00–R99)

Using the alphabetic and tabular references, locate the following conditions and code to acceptable specificity, three to seven characters. Observe the coding instructions and include codes from other chapters as directed.

Diagnoses		ICD-10-CM	ICD-9-CM
1.	Severe staphylococcal sepsis with shock	_____	_____
2.	Periumbilical pain	_____	_____
3.	Vertigo	_____	_____
4.	Elevated blood pressure, no hypertension	_____	_____
5.	Abnormal cervical Pap smear	_____	_____
6.	Headache	_____	_____
7.	Chronic peritoneal effusion	_____	_____
8.	Excessive crying, 12-day-old infant	_____	_____
9.	Intellectual functioning at borderline level	_____	_____
10.	Localized edema, right foot	_____	_____
11.	Flatulence	_____	_____
12.	Postnasal drip	_____	_____
13.	Fasciculations of lower extremities	_____	_____
14.	Hemoptysis	_____	_____
15.	Frequent blushing	_____	_____
16.	Swelling of the right side of the neck	_____	_____
17.	Physical debility from old age	_____	_____
18.	Functional urinary incontinence	_____	_____
19.	Cardiorespiratory failure	_____	_____
20.	Chronic fatigue syndrome	_____	_____
21.	Skin induration	_____	_____
22.	Abnormal EEG	_____	_____
23.	Persistent vegetative state	_____	_____
24.	Postimmunization fever	_____	_____
25.	Painful urination	_____	_____

Name _____

Injury, Poisoning, and Certain Other Consequences of External Causes (S00–T88)

When coding **Chapter 19**, review and observe all notes, instructions, and exclusions. These codes frequently require a code from another Chapter.

This chapter contains the following blocks:

S00–S09	Injuries to the head
S10–S19	Injuries to the neck
S20–S29	Injuries to the thorax
S30–S39	Injuries to the abdomen, lower back, lumbar spine, pelvis, and external genitals
S40–S49	Injuries to the shoulder and upper arm
S50–S59	Injuries to the elbow and forearm
S60–S69	Injuries to the wrist, hand, and fingers
S70–S79	Injuries to the hip and thigh
S80–S89	Injuries to the knee and lower leg
S90–S99	Injuries to the ankle and foot
T07	Injuries involving multiple body regions
T14	Injury to unspecified body region
T15–T19	Effects of foreign body entering through natural orifice
T20–T25	Burns and corrosions of external body surface, specified by site
T26–T28	Burns and corrosions confined to eye and internal organs
T30–T32	Burns and corrosions of multiple and unspecified body regions
T33–T34	Frostbite
T36–T50	Poisoning by or adverse effect of an underdosing of drugs, medicaments, and biological substances
T51–T65	Toxic effects of substances chiefly nonmedicinal as to source
T66–T78	Other and unspecified effects of external causes
T79	Certain early complications of trauma
T80–T88	Complications of surgical and medical care, not elsewhere classified

There are additional instructions within each block of codes, advising "includes," "Excludes 1," "Excludes 2," "code first," "code also," or "use additional code." Code only what is stated or known in the medical record. If no additional information is provided in the worksheet, code only the specific term(s).

Name _____

Using the blocks on the previous page as guidance, locate the three-character categories for the following diagnoses:

Diagnoses	ICD-10-CM	ICD-9-CM
1. Scalp laceration with foreign body	_____	_____
2. New bucket-handle tear, right medial meniscus	_____	_____
3. Death from concussion with no return to consciousness	_____	_____
4. Aero-otitis media	_____	_____
5. Fracture of lumbosacral vertebra	_____	_____
6. Rejection of bone marrow transplant	_____	_____
7. Nondisplaced fracture, body of left scapula	_____	_____
8. First-degree burn of elbow, right	_____	_____
9. Superficial frostbite of the nose	_____	_____
10. Posterior arch fracture, first cervical vertebra	_____	_____

Name _____

Injury, Poisoning, and Certain Other Consequences of External Causes (S00–T88)

Using the alphabetic and tabular references, locate the following conditions and code to acceptable specificity, three to seven characters. Observe the coding instructions and include codes from other chapters as directed. Unless otherwise specified, all encounters are "initial."

	Diagnoses	ICD-10-CM	ICD-9-CM
1.	Lump from nonvenomous insect bite, 1 year ago, right breast	_____	_____
2.	Rejection of lung transplant	_____	_____
3.	Seen again for nonunion, torus fracture, left lower fibula	_____	_____
4.	ER visit for Type IIIA open fracture, left femur neck	_____	_____
5.	Foreign body, left cornea	_____	_____
6.	Left ankle sprain	_____	_____
7.	Patient admitted for mechanical breakdown of mitral valve prosthesis	_____	_____
8.	Cervical spine nerve root injury	_____	_____
9.	Per police report and confirmed by physician: Elderly patient abused by home health care worker	_____	_____
10.	Black eye, right, follow up visit	_____	_____
11.	Fracture mandibular ramus, healing well	_____	_____
12.	Foreign body (stone) in left nostril	_____	_____
13.	Continuing care for healing subluxation L4/L5 vertebra	_____	_____
14.	Rash at site of immunization	_____	_____
15.	ER visit, suicide attempt with aspirin	_____	_____
16.	Third degree burn, left palm	_____	_____
17.	Traumatic partial amputation right ear, 20 minutes ago	_____	_____
18.	Necrotic frostbite, left ear	_____	_____
19.	Seen for sequelae of toxic cobra venom	_____	_____
20.	Follow-up visit for healing nasal bone fracture	_____	_____
21.	Follow-up visit for previous allergic reaction	_____	_____
22.	Accidental poisoning by shellfish	_____	_____
23.	Crush injury, right great toe	_____	_____
24.	Seen for left shoulder puncture with foreign body	_____	_____
25.	Seen in ER for esophageal burn from coffee she drank	_____	_____

Name _____

External Causes of Morbidity (V00–Y99)

Chapter 20 has extensive notes on the proper use of these codes with other chapter conditions. Observe all Chapter 20 instructions and guidelines. These codes replace the "E" codes of ICD-9-CM. Use of these codes may point to billing a liability carrier or auto insurance rather than the patient's private health insurance. Although the federal government does not require use of external cause codes, some payers and state agencies require the use of these specialized codes. Detailed guidelines are provided for the four main categories of external cause codes:

1. External cause of injury (such as fall, burn, assault)

2. Place of occurrence (home, school, hotel, football field)

3. Activity (swimming, skiing, skating)

4. External cause status (military, civilian, volunteer)

This chapter contains the following blocks:

V00–Y09	Pedestrian injured in transport accident
V10–V19	Pedal cycle rider injured in transport accident
V20–V29	Motorcycle rider injured in transport accident
V30–V39	Occupant of three-wheeled motor vehicle injured in transport accident
V40–V49	Car occupant injured in transport accident
V50–V59	Occupant of pick-up truck or van injured in transport accident
V60–V69	Occupant of heavy transport vehicle injured in transport accident
V70–V79	Bus occupant injured in transport accident
V80–V89	Other land transport accidents
V90–V94	Water transport accidents
V95–V97	Air and space transport accidents
V98–V99	Other and unspecified transport accidents
W00–X58	Other external causes of accidental injury
W00–W19	Slipping, tripping, stumbling and falls
W20–W49	Exposure to inanimate mechanical forces
W50–W64	Exposure to animate mechanical forces
W65–W74	Accidental non-transport drowning and submersion
W85–W99	Exposure to electric current, radiation and extreme ambient air temperature and pressure
X00–X08	Exposure to smoke, fire and flames
X10–X19	Contact with heat and hot substances
X30–X39	Exposure to forces of nature
X52–X58	Accidental exposure to other specified factors
X71–X83	Intentional self-harm
X92–Y08	Assault
Y21–Y33	Event of undetermined intent
Y35–Y38	Legal intervention, operations of war, military operations, and terrorism

Name _____

Y62–Y84	Complications of medical and surgical care
Y62–Y69	Misadventures to patients during surgical and medical care
Y70–Y82	Medical devices associated with adverse incidents in diagnostic and therapeutic use
Y83–Y84	Surgical and other medical procedures as the cause of abnormal reaction of the patient, or of later complication, without mention of misadventure at the time of the procedure
Y90–Y99	Supplementary factors related to causes of morbidity classified elsewhere

Code only what is stated or known in the medical record. If no additional information is provided in the worksheet, code only the specific term(s).

Using the blocks on the previous page as guidance, locate the three-character categories for the following diagnoses:

	Diagnoses	ICD-10-CM	ICD-9-CM
1.	Snowboarder collided with a tree	_____	_____
2.	Two dune buggies collided, one passenger injured	_____	_____
3.	Paper cut	_____	_____
4.	Bystander injured when police used tear gas	_____	_____
5.	Right leg amputated: wrong leg	_____	_____
6.	Injured while running with scissors	_____	_____
7.	Bitten by a macaw	_____	_____
8.	Toddler fell out when grocery cart tipped over	_____	_____
9.	Injured when a small plane hit his car	_____	_____
10.	Runner injured in Boston Marathon bombing	_____	_____

Name _____

External Causes of Morbidity (V00–Y99)

Using the alphabetic and tabular references, locate the following conditions and code to acceptable specificity, three to seven characters. Observe the coding instructions and include the location and activity codes (Y92–Y93) if applicable for initial service and documented. For this exercise, we will not be assigning codes from the external cause status (Y99.0–Y99.9) These codes may not be used as the principle diagnosis and may not be required at present. All are the "initial encounter."

Diagnoses	ICD-10-CM External Injury Code	Location/ Activity
1. Nanny with a baby stroller was injured by a bicyclist in the park	_____	_____
2. Struck by baseball at high school home game	_____	_____
3. Injured in an avalanche	_____	_____
4. Armored car driver injured in collision with a cow (nontraffic accident)	_____	_____
5. Injured in his garage workshop by his radial saw. Patient lives in a single-family home.	_____	_____
6. Driver of fork lift injured in a warehouse accident	_____	_____
7. Foster mother neglected and mistreated the toddler	_____	_____
8. Patient was injured as a passenger in a snowmobile accident (nontraffic)	_____	_____
9. Patient was a passenger on a bus and was injured when the bus collided with a pick-up truck	_____	_____
10. Sawed off ring causing constriction to her finger	_____	_____
11. Bitten by an orca while surfing in the ocean at a local beach	_____	_____
12. Fell from icy steps at local grocery store	_____	_____
13. Patient was injured as a result of a helicopter crash	_____	_____
14. Burned when the kayak caught fire on the river	_____	_____
15. Dove into the lake, struck the bottom, and drowned	_____	_____
16. Child accidentally drowned, left alone in bathtub. Accident occurred in a single-family home.	_____	_____
17. Canoer hurt when hit by motorboat on river	_____	_____
18. Became ill from smoke and fumes when his apartment caught fire	_____	_____
19. Patient sustained an injury of his left hand by a ball while playing racquetball	_____	_____

Name _____

20. Injuries occurred when he fell off the toilet at his apartment   _____   _____

21. Bulldozer driver injured when earth collapsed under him   _____   _____

22. Child hurt when IED exploded; war souvenir from Iraq   _____   _____

23. Injured from exposure to tanning bed   _____   _____

24. Was assaulted and struck by a hockey stick   _____   _____

25. Fell asleep smoking, setting hotel sofa on fire   _____   _____

Factors Influencing Health Status and Contact with Health Services (Z00–Z99)

Chapter 21 begins with an explanation that these codes represent reasons for encounters and that a corresponding procedure code must accompany a Z code if a procedure from other chapters is performed. Review and observe all notes, exclusions, and chapter guidelines when coding this chapter. One of the major changes between ICD-9-CM and ICD-10-CM deals with aftercare of fractures. Note the Excludes 1 code under category Z47 that explains that aftercare for healing fracture is coded to fracture with the 7th character "D." These codes expand the "V" codes in ICD-9-CM.

This chapter contains the following blocks:

Z00–Z13	Persons encountering health service for examinations
Z14–Z15	Genetic carrier and genetic susceptibility to disease
Z16	Resistance to antimicrobial drugs
Z17	Estrogen receptor status
Z18	Retained foreign body fragments
Z20–Z28	Persons with potential health hazards related to communicable diseases
Z30–Z39	Persons encountering health services in circumstances related to reproduction
Z40–Z53	Encounters for other specific health care
Z55–Z65	Persons with potential health hazards related to socioeconomic and psychosocial circumstances
Z66	Do not resuscitate status
Z67	Blood type
Z68	Body mass index (BMI)
Z69–Z76	Persons encountering health services in other circumstances
Z77–Z99	Persons with potential health hazards related to family and personal history and certain conditions influencing health status

There are additional instructions within each block of codes advising "includes," "Excludes 1," "Excludes 2," "code first," "code also," or "use additional code." Code only what is stated or known in the medical record. If no additional information is provided in the worksheet, code only the specific term(s).

Name _____

Using the blocks on the previous page as guidance, locate the three-character categories for the following diagnoses:

		ICD-10-CM	ICD-9-CM
1.	Physical exam for summer camp	_____	_____
2.	Seen for suture removal	_____	_____
3.	Family history of alcohol dependence/abuse	_____	_____
4.	Encounter for exam of ears and hearing evaluation	_____	_____
5.	Has used insulin for the past 22 years	_____	_____
6.	Visit to enroll patient in palliative care	_____	_____
7.	Personal history of thrombophlebitis	_____	_____
8.	Immunization declined based on religion	_____	_____
9.	Empty nest syndrome	_____	_____
10.	Seen for consideration of breast implants	_____	_____

Name _____

Factors Influencing Health Status and Contact with Health Services (Z00–Z99)

Using the alphabetic and tabular references, locate the following conditions and code to acceptable specificity, three to seven characters. Observe the coding instructions and chapter-specific guidelines. These are initial visits unless otherwise specified. Include codes from other chapters, as directed, if that information is included.

	Diagnoses	ICD-10-CM	ICD-9-CM
1.	Routine GYN exam, without abnormal findings	_____	_____
2.	Encounter for postmastectomy breast reconstruction	_____	_____
3.	Seen for inability to get along with boss and workmates	_____	_____
4.	Type O blood, Rh negative	_____	_____
5.	Has Alzheimer's and needs continuous supervision	_____	_____
6.	Encounter for pregnancy test with positive result	_____	_____
7.	Type A behavior pattern	_____	_____
8.	Genetic susceptibility to breast cancer	_____	_____
9.	Gastric bypass status for obesity	_____	_____
10.	Observation for suspected ingestion of poison, ruled out	_____	_____
11.	Had polio as a child	_____	_____
12.	Personal history of basal and squamous cell carcinoma	_____	_____
13.	Seen to screen for diabetes mellitus	_____	_____
14.	Visit to fit and adjust artificial left eye	_____	_____
15.	Patient seen in outpatient physical therapy department after suffering a communited fracture of the left radial shaft	_____	_____
16.	Adult body mass index: 23.5	_____	_____
17.	Issuing repeat prescriptions for a chronic disease	_____	_____
18.	Patient seen in the office for removal of surgical drain	_____	_____
19.	Adjustment of gastric lap band	_____	_____
20.	Contact with and exposure to asbestos	_____	_____
21.	Patient has resistance to ampicillin	_____	_____
22.	Patient seen for insulin pump fitting and training	_____	_____
23.	Status post total hysterectomy	_____	_____
24.	Visit to screen for chlamydia	_____	_____
25.	Allergic to shellfish	_____	_____

Name _____

UNIT V PUTTING IT ALL TOGETHER

This series of case studies asks you to find the correct procedure and diagnosis codes. Note also that you are asked to include any required modifier. The answers and the rationale for the answer follow this section. Read the case studies carefully, look for key terms, and be certain to follow all coding rules from CPT, HCPCS, and ICD-10-CM. Do not assign ICD-10-CM External Cause codes for this exercise (codes beginning with V, W, X, and Y). List the procedures and modifiers in the order they would appear on the claim form (1–4) and list the corresponding diagnoses that supports medical necessity with numbers 1–4.

1. The patient has an unstable left keratoconus. He can no longer keep his contact lenses in place. The surgeon performed an anterior lamellar keratoplasty.

   Proc/Mod   1 _____   ICD-10-CM   1 _____

   2 _____   2 _____

   3 _____   3 _____

   4 _____   4 _____

2. A 22-year-old male was admitted to a residential psychiatric facility for treatment of an exacerbation of Asperger's syndrome. Following a comprehensive workup, he had 30 minutes of biofeedback psychotherapy on the day of admission.

   Proc/Mod   1 _____   ICD-10-CM   1 _____

   2 _____   2 _____

   3 _____   3 _____

   4 _____   4 _____

3. The physician admitted the patient to a nursing facility and performed a detailed history and physical examination with medical decision making of low complexity. The patient has had a significant recovery from his left-sided paralysis following a stroke. Since he is right-handed, he can now feed and dress himself. The physician documents the diagnosis of mild residual monoplegia of the left lower leg.

   Proc/Mod   1 _____   ICD-10-CM   1 _____

   2 _____   2 _____

   3 _____   3 _____

   4 _____   4 _____

Name _____

4. The orthopedic surgeon discharges the patient from the hospital following a right total hip replacement for osteoarthritis.

Proc/Mod   1 _____   ICD-10-CM   1 _____

          2 _____   2 _____

          3 _____   3 _____

          4 _____   4 _____

5. Patient presents to the physician's office after injuring his left thumb. The doctor took two x-ray views of the left thumb. The x-ray revealed no fracture; therefore, the physician treated the sprain injury by strapping the thumb with one yard of 3-inch elastic compression bandage.

Proc/Mod   1 _____   ICD-10-CM   1 _____

          2 _____   2 _____

          3 _____   3 _____

          4 _____   4 _____

6. A patient, age 87, was scheduled at Metropolitan Hospital for outpatient surgery to replace his mature right cortical cataract with a lens implant. Just as Dr. Florez was to begin the procedure, the patient developed a significant cardiac dysrhythmia. The surgery was canceled, and Dr. Florez admitted the patient to the hospital's observation unit for care of the arrhythmia. Dr. Connick, a cardiologist, later that day admitted the patient to Metropolitan Hospital for a complete cardiac workup.

Code the services of Dr. Florez.

Proc/Mod   1 _____   ICD-10-CM   1 _____

          2 _____   2 _____

          3 _____   3 _____

          4 _____   4 _____

7. An ambulance brought a 37-year-old man to the Central City Hospital ER after he was injured in a hit-and-run accident. The orthopedic surgeon, Dr. Gupta, treated the patient in the emergency department for the following nondisplaced fractures: metacarpal, right ring finger; a mandible on the right; and the closed treatment of a fractured right femur shaft. When the patient was stable, Dr. Jones admitted him to Central City Hospital for continuing care of the fractures. Code Dr. Gupta's services.

Proc/Mod   1 _____   ICD-10-CM   1 _____

          2 _____   2 _____

          3 _____   3 _____

          4 _____   4 _____

Name _____

8. A physician discharged the 79-year-old female patient from the observation unit of Mercy Medical Center after she recovered from an acute exacerbation from severe persistent asthma. She was seen earlier that afternoon in his office for the asthma attack and was immediately transported to the hospital. The patient only required a one-day stay (same date) and the physician provided a comprehensive history and examination and medical decision making was of moderate complexity.

Proc/Mod	1 _____	ICD-10-CM	1 _____
	2 _____		2 _____
	3 _____		3 _____
	4 _____		4 _____

9. The 4-year-old child was seen by her pediatrician after she had been ill for two days with a productive cough and now had developed a fever. Her last visit was six months ago. Her examination focused on the presenting problems with low medical decision making. The doctor diagnosis is documented as acute bronchitis.

Proc/Mod	1 _____	ICD-10-CM	1 _____
	2 _____		2 _____
	3 _____		3 _____
	4 _____		4 _____

10. The patient, who has Type 2 diabetes and severe osteoarthritis, was seen in the office to discuss his recent lab work for glucose levels. When he appeared uncoordinated and confused, the physician performed a glucose test with a reagent strip that showed the patient's glucose level was low. The patient was given crackers and a drink and later re-tested with the reagent strip. The physician became concerned that the patient was not taking his medications correctly or perhaps had developed a new problem, so he ordered a comprehensive metabolic panel to be performed at the local hospital. The physician performed a detailed history and examination, and the decision making was of moderate complexity. The physician documents the diagnosis as Type 2 DM with hypoglycemia.

Proc/Mod	1 _____	ICD-10-CM	1 _____
	2 _____		2 _____
	3 _____		3 _____
	4 _____		4 _____

Name _____

11. Patient was seen in the outpatient surgery department for abdominal pain. The surgeon performed a colonoscopy to the cecum and biopsied several sites in the descending and transverse colon. The physician documents the diagnosis of diverticulosis of the descending colon. Code for the surgeon's services.

Proc/Mod   1 _____   ICD-10-CM   1 _____

2 _____   2 _____

3 _____   3 _____

4 _____   4 _____

12. A patient returned to his cardiologist's office for a six-month recheck of the medications for his hypertensive heart disease. A routine EKG was performed that showed some abnormalities; therefore, a further diagnostic workup was scheduled. The doctor's physician assistant supervised the test and prepared the tracing for cardiologist's interpretation. The documentation supports an expanded problem focused history and physical examination with medical decision making of moderate complexity.

Proc/Mod   1 _____   ICD-10-CM   1 _____

2 _____   2 _____

3 _____   3 _____

4 _____   4 _____

13. A male patient was seen in his family doctor's office after suffering a bee sting. The physician treated the patient with a stinging insect venom injection to prevent anaphylaxis. The physician documented the diagnosis of bee sting.

Proc/Mod   1 _____   ICD-10-CM   1 _____

2 _____   2 _____

3 _____   3 _____

4 _____   4 _____

14. The patient was seen in the Emergency Department after having scrap metal pieces thrown in his right eye. He had no change in vision but did have a small laceration in the cheek area. Films in the emergency department revealed a metal foreign body embedded in the right lower eyelid just above the laceration. The 2.0 cm superficial cheek laceration was sutured and the foreign body removed by the ER physician. The patient was advised to see his primary care physician for follow-up care. The documentation supports an expanded problem focused history and examination with moderate medical decision making.

Proc/Mod   1 _____   ICD-10-CM   1 _____

2 _____   2 _____

3 _____   3 _____

4 _____   4 _____

Name _____

15. A 37-year-old new patient was seen in the office for trauma to the left elbow received after a fall. X-rays (two views) of the elbow revealed no fracture. The patient was advised to rest the arm and use hot or cold compresses for the swelling. He was asked to contact the office if the arm was not better in a few days. The E/M service is supported by documentation of an expanded problem focused history and examination with medical decision making of low complexity. The physician documents the diagnosis of contusion of left elbow.

Proc/Mod   1 _____   ICD-10-CM   1 _____

           2 _____   2 _____

           3 _____   3 _____

           4 _____   4 _____

16. A pediatrician in solo practice performed a routine newborn exam. Later that day the baby developed respiratory distress and was transferred to the care of a neonatologist, who admitted the baby to the neonatal intensive care unit (NICU). What diagnosis and services would be reported for the pediatrician?

Proc/Mod   1 _____   ICD-10-CM   1 _____

           2 _____   2 _____

           3 _____   3 _____

           4 _____   4 _____

17. The client was seen in a full 60-minute psychotherapy visit for chronic posttraumatic stress disorder.

Proc/Mod   1 _____   ICD-10-CM   1 _____

           2 _____   2 _____

           3 _____   3 _____

           4 _____   4 _____

18. A physician left her group practice and established an office in the next town. Some of her patients followed her to the new practice. She set up new records for these patients and incorporated copies from the group practice records into these charts. She saw a patient from her prior practice with documentation of an expanded problem focused history and examination with moderate decision making visit for the six-month renewal of his prescriptions for Type 2 diabetes.

Proc/Mod   1 _____   ICD-10-CM   1 _____

           2 _____   2 _____

           3 _____   3 _____

           4 _____   4 _____

Name _____

19.   The 13-year-old patient had an abscess on the right middle finger and a sebaceous cyst of
      the left first toe. Both lesions were treated by I & D at the same operative session.

      Proc/Mod   1 _____   ICD-10-CM   1 _____

                  2 _____   2 _____

                  3 _____   3 _____

                  4 _____   4 _____

20.   The patient had complained of occasional rectal bleeding over the past year. He was
      scheduled for a diagnostic flexible sigmoidoscopy. The surgeon also removed three
      polyps using a snare. All lesions were proximal to the splenic flexure in the descending
      colon.

      Proc/Mod   1 _____   ICD-10-CM   1 _____

                  2 _____   2 _____

                  3 _____   3 _____

                  4 _____   4 _____

21.   The patient was seen for worsening knee pain for the past year. The surgeon performed
      a diagnostic arthroscopy with a partial medial meniscectomy and chondroplasty of the
      right knee for osteochondritis.

      Proc/Mod   1 _____   ICD-10-CM   1 _____

                  2 _____   2 _____

                  3 _____   3 _____

                  4 _____   4 _____

22.   The 22-year-old female patient is seen in the clinic with the diagnosis of missed
      abortion, at 19 weeks. The surgeon performed a D&C and subsequently delivered all the
      products of conception.

      Proc/Mod   1 _____   ICD-10-CM   1 _____

                  2 _____   2 _____

                  3 _____   3 _____

                  4 _____   4 _____

Current Procedural Terminology ©2014 American Medical Association. All Rights Reserved.

Name _____

23. The patient had not seen the physician for two years when he returned to the office concerned about some "red bumps" on his face, neck, and arms. Documentation supports an expanded problem focused history and examination with straightforward medical decision making. The physician diagnosed the "bumps" as actinic keratoses. The doctor also removed a skin tag from the neck or shoulder area where it had been irritated by the patient's shirt collars.

Proc/Mod	1	_____	ICD-10-CM	1	_____
	2	_____		2	_____
	3	_____		3	_____
	4	_____		4	_____

24. A 41-year-old patient was admitted for abdominal pain due to gallstones. The surgeon performed a laparoscopic cholecystectomy. The diagnosis was documented as acute and chronic cholecystitis with cholelithiasis.

Proc/Mod	1	_____	ICD-10-CM	1	_____
	2	_____		2	_____
	3	_____		3	_____
	4	_____		4	_____

25. An 18-month child is seen in the office for varicella virus vaccine administered subcutaneously. The nurse practitioner provided counselling about the vaccine and answered the mother's questions and addressed her concerns.

Proc/Mod	1	_____	ICD-10-CM	1	_____
	2	_____		2	_____
	3	_____		3	_____
	4	_____		4	_____

Putting It All Together—Answers and Rationales

1. Proc/Mod: 1) 65710   Diagnosis: 1) H18.622

    The CPT code is in the eye section. In ICD-10-CM, the subterm unstable is listed under the main term Keratoconus.

2. Proc/Mod: 1) 99305, 2) 90875   Diagnosis: 1) F84.5, 2) F84.5

    CPT states that medical psychotherapy, when performed, is reported in addition to the E/M service.

3. Proc/Mod: 1) 99304   Diagnosis: 1) I69.344

    The physician's documentation supports an E/M code of 99304. Coding guideline (Chapter 9, D - Sequela of cerebrovascular disease) provides guidance for classifying the late effect of a neurologic deficit that persists after initial onset. The nursing facility will provide rehabilitation for the patient's residual monoplegia.

4. Proc/Mod: 1) 27130-RT   Diagnosis: 1) M16.11

    This is a straightforward example of a surgical billing. There is no medical care reported by the surgeon, as all related medical care is included in the surgical procedure.

5. Proc/Mod: 1) 73120-LT, 2) 29280-FA, 3) A6449 q=1   Diagnosis: 1-3) S63.682A

    When reporting strapping, remember to include the required supplies. In this case, a fracture was not confirmed. Note that ICD-10-CM has specific codes for a sprain of the left thumb with initial encounter identified by the final character.

6. Proc/Mod: 1) 99235   Diagnosis: 1) H25.011, I49.9

    Evaluation and Management code 99235, rather than 99219, is correct because Dr. Florez admitted and discharged (by a transfer of care) the patient on the same day. Dr. Connick will report the initial hospital care service, 99221-99223. The diagnosis codes reported for Dr. Florez would be the cataract first and arrhythmia second. "When a patient presents for outpatient surgery and develops complications requiring admission to observation, code the reason for the surgery as the first reported diagnosis (reason for the encounter) followed by codes for the complications as secondary diagnoses." (Guidelines, Section IV, A 2)

7. Proc/Mod: 1) 27500, 2) 21450-RT, 3) 26600-F8   Diagnosis: 1) S72.301A,

                                                                     2) S02.609A, 3) S62.304A

    Remember to put the most significant surgery on the first line of the claim, regardless of how they are listed on the operative note. Most computer software programs will provide guidance on appropriate listing of codes. Since the descriptions did not refer to a manipulation and the fractures were nondisplaced, use codes that state "no manipulation." Modifier –51 may be required by the payer on the second and third services as well as the modifier describing the finger. Mandible diagnosis code will be "unspecified" since the specific location was not identified; the metacarpal and the shaft of the femur are identified and coded by site.

8. Proc/Mod: 1) 99235 Diagnosis: 1) J45.51

The office visit is not billed as those services are related to the hospital observation admission of the same day (see the note before code 99234 in CPT). The diagnosis reflects the severity of the illness.

9. Proc/Mod: 1) 99212 Diagnosis: 1) J20.9

The patient is established since she was seen six months ago. The E/M code requires two of the three key components; therefore code 99212 is reported for this service. The symptoms of cough and fever would not be reported since the definitive diagnosis of bronchitis was established (see Guideline IV.D).

10. Proc/Mod: 1) 99214, 2) 82948, 3) 82948-91 Diagnosis: 1–3) E11.649

The documentation for an established patient meets all three key components. The repeat lab test in the office requires modifier –91. The metabolic panel was ordered, not performed in the office. The osteoarthritis was not treated on this visit, so the code is not included. The symptoms of uncoordinated and confused relate to the diagnosis of diabetes with hypoglycemia; therefore, would not be assigned as separate codes.

11. Proc/Mod: 1) 45380 Diagnosis: 1) K57.30

The CPT code for a biopsy of the colon includes single or multiple. The specific code for diverticulosis of the large intestine should be reported.

12. Proc/Mod: 1) 99213-25, 2) 93000 Diagnosis: 1–2) I11.9

The established patient visit required two of the three key components to support the CPT code 99213. The use of modifier 25 explains that there was an E/M service performed beyond the EKG procedure. The ICD-10-CM code I11.9 is assigned for hypertensive heart disease without heart failure.

13. Proc/Mod: 1) 95130 Diagnosis: 1) T63.441A

It is important to note that the physician would have to document separate identifiable services, in addition to the injection, in order to report an E/M code. See the instructional note before CPT code 95115. Note that the ICD-10-CM code assumes the sting was unintentional as most people who are allergic to bees try to avoid them.

14. Proc/Mod: 1) 67938-E4, 2) 12011 3) 99283-25 Diagnosis: 1) S01.121A

2) S01.411A 3) both ICD-10-CM codes relate to the E/M service.

Since the removal of an embedded foreign body is the major procedure, it should be reported first. Computer software programs will assist with determining the order on an electronic claim. Modifier –25 explains that E/M services were performed beyond the surgical repair and removal of foreign body. ICD-10-CM codes for the embedded foreign body and laceration of the cheek correspond to the applicable CPT code to explain the reason for the service. Note that the "A" on each diagnosis code indicates this was the initial service.

15.   Proc/Mod: 1) 99202-25, 2) 73070-LT   Diagnosis: 1–2) S50.02xA

The documentation for a new patient requires three of the key components; therefore, code 99202 is reported. The modifier –25 is appended to the E/M code to state that separate services were performed beyond taking the x-ray. Since there was no fracture or open wound, the diagnosis must be contusion for the first two services. The "A" indicates this is the first service for that diagnosis.

16.   Proc/Mod: 1) 99460   Diagnosis: 1) Z00.110

The pediatrician's service was the newborn exam and is billable since he is not in practice with the neonatologist. The diagnosis, at the time of his visit, would have been a normal newborn examination. The problem occurred later.

17.   Proc/Mod: 1) 90837   Diagnosis: 1) F43.12

There is no documentation to support a separate E/M service; therefore, only the psychotherapy code is reported. The diagnosis could be reported as PTSD, chronic (F43.12)

18.   Proc/Mod: 1) 99213   Diagnosis: 1) E11.9

Assuming that she was the doctor who prescribed the meds six months ago, this would be an established patient visit. If the patient is transferring to her practice and had no professional services in the past three years from this physician or another physician of the same specialty in her former practice, this would be a new patient visit, 99202. The change in tax identification numbers and establishing a new chart does not make this a new patient visit. ICD-10-CM code E11.9 classifies Type 2 diabetes mellitus.

19.   Proc/Mod: 1) 10061-F7-TA   Diagnosis: 1) L02.511, L72.3

Do not report two codes, 10060-F7 and 10060-TA (unless instructed to do so by the payer) as the description for 10061 states "multiple." Code 10061 would be the correct procedure code even though the treatment areas are separate. Using both modifiers and two diagnosis codes may result in an adequate payment, but if it doesn't, that reporting could help with the appeal.

20.   Proc/Mod: 1) 45338   Diagnosis: 1) D12.4

CPT states: "surgical endoscopy always includes diagnostic endoscopy." Code 45338 is used once regardless of the number of polyps removed. The diagnosis should be polyp of the colon rather than rectal bleeding. As there is no mention of malignancy, be certain you select diagnosis codes from the benign section.

21.   Proc/Mod: 1) 29881-RT   Diagnosis: 1) M17.11

The CPT code description states meniscectomy, medial or lateral. In the Alphabetic Index of ICD-10-CM, the subterm osteochondritis states to *see also* "osteochondropathy, by site." Under osteochondropathy of the knee joint is a reference to see "osteoarthritis, primary, knee."

22.   Proc/Mod: 1) 59821   Diagnosis: 1) O02.1

Note that the procedure code includes all the visits associated with the abortion and D&C service.

23. Proc/Mod: 1) 99213-25, 2) 11200   Diagnosis: 1) L57.0, 2) L91.8

The documentation meets two of the three key elements for code 99213. Modifier –25 explains that E/M services were provided beyond the surgical services. The visit was more complex than the usual preoperative evaluation and postoperative care for a single skin tag with the finding of actinic keratoses. Use codes L57.0 for the office visit, and L91.8 for the surgical service.

24. Proc/Mod: 1) 47562   Diagnosis: 1) K80.12

The removal of the gallbladder was performed laparoscopically. The ICD-10-CM code is a combination code that includes the gallstones with acute and chronic cholecystitis. There was no mention of obstruction.

25. Proc/Mod: 1) 90460 2) 90716   Diagnosis: 1–2) Z23

Since counselling was provided, CPT code 90460 would be reported in addition to the code for the vaccine. There were no E/M services documented in this case. The ICD-10-CM code reflects that the visit was for immunization.

UNIT VI EXAM QUESTIONS FOR CPT, CPT AND HCPCS, AND ICD-10-CM

Directions:

- Use the appropriate coding manual to determine the correct choice for each situation.
- Answer sheet is provided at the end of each exam for recording your choice for each question.

Name _____

Exam Questions for CPT

Directions: Use the appropriate coding manual to determine the correct choice for each situation.

1. The patient underwent nerve grafting of the right foot, 3 cm.

   ① 64885-RT

   ② 64890-RT

   ③ 64891-RT

   ④ 64901-RT

2. Surgeon performed a thyroidectomy for removal of remaining thyroid tissue after previous right lobectomy for suspected malignancy.

   ① 60225

   ② 60240

   ③ 60260

   ④ 60270

3. A patient, who is a resident of a nursing facility, was seen for annual assessment. What category of code(s) would be referenced for selecting a code?

   ① 99315–99316

   ② 99307–99310

   ③ 99318

   ④ 99339–33340

4. An 81-year-old patient receives anesthesia prior to undergoing cardioversion for persistent, life threatening arrhythmia. Include physical status modifier with code.

   ① 00400-P2 + 99100

   ② 00410-P3 + 99140

   ③ 00410-P2 + 99100

   ④ 00410-P4 + 99100

5. Surgeon performs a sphenoid sinusotomy for removal of polyps, including biopsy.

   ① 31020

   ② 31050

   ③ 31051

   ④ 31070

6. Physician performs a surgical ligation of the common carotid artery.

   ① 37600

   ② 37605

   ③ 37606

   ④ 37615

7. A 67-year-old patient underwent contact laser vaporization of the prostate.

   ① 52450

   ② 52601

   ③ 52647

   ④ 52648

8. The patient underwent total abdominal hysterectomy, sparing the tubes and ovaries.

   ① 58150

   ② 58152

   ③ 58200

   ④ 58210

9. Radiologist directs and interprets the placement of a long gastrostomy tube in a patient who is status post cerebrovascular accident.

   ① 43246-26

   ② 74340

   ③ 74355

   ④ 74363

10. A nursing home patient was admitted for management of pneumonia, which is now resolved. The physician came by the facility to discharge the patient home, spending 20 minutes with the patient and family.

    ① 99217

    ② 99238

    ③ 99315

    ④ 99339

11. The physician conducted an initial office consultation for a 44-year-old patient, 6 years status post lumbar laminectomy with intractable sciatic pain, depression, and history of narcotic dependency or abuse. The physician performs a comprehensive history and examination with medical decision making of high complexity.

    ① 99241

    ② 99243

    ③ 99244

    ④ 99245

12. A 16-year-old patient undergoes excision of an aneurysmal bone cyst of the proximal right humerus, with allograft.

    ① 23155

    ② 23156

    ③ 23184

    ④ 23220

13. A 15-year-old, otherwise healthy patient receives anesthesia for electroconvulsive therapy. Include physical status modifier with code.

    ① 00104-P1

    ② 00104-P2

    ③ 00190-P1

    ④ 00210-P1

14. A patient, who is status post cochlear implant, has a visit for group rehabilitation, treatment of speech, and a processing disorder.

    ① 92507

    ② 92508

    ③ 92520

    ④ 92557

15. Health care employee receives the first of three hepatitis B vaccinations IM from her doctor.

    ① 90371 + 96372

    ② 90746 + 90471

    ③ 90746 + 96372

    ④ 96372

16. The surgeon performed a cervical conization with loop electrical excision of the transitional zone.

    ① 57460

    ② 57500

    ③ 57520

    ④ 57522

17. The patient had a stereotactic biopsy of intracranial lesion under MR guidance.

    ① 61720

    ② 61750

    ③ 61751

    ④ 61770

18. The physician counsels a group of teenagers regarding sexually transmitted diseases and prevention. Session lasts 30 minutes.

    ① 99401

    ② 99402

    ③ 99411

    ④ 99411-26

19. The ED physician examines an 18-year-old in the emergency department for recurrent, severe menstrual migraine headache. The physician performs a problem-focused history and examination with straight-forward decision making.

① 99241

② 99281

③ 99282

④ 99284

20. The patient had an in-office simple incision and drainage of a pilonidal cyst.

① 10060

② 10061

③ 10080

④ 10081

21. The Emergency Department physician repaired superficial lacerations of the chin (2.0 cm) and cheek (3.0 cm).

① 12011 + 12013

② 12013

③ 12051 + 12052

④ 12052

22. A patient with a congenital cleft palate, underwent a rhinoplasty with columellar lengthening, including the septum and tip.

① 30410

② 30430

③ 30460

④ 30462

23. A 34-year-old patient suspected of having sleep apnea had a sleep study with recording of ventilation, respiratory effort, heart rate, and oxygen saturation. A technologist was in attendance.

① 95805

② 95806

③ 95807

④ 95811

24. Surgeon performed excision of pterygium with grafting, left eye.

① 65400

② 65420-LT

③ 65426-LT

④ 66999

25. The neonatologist was asked to be on standby for 35 minutes for cesarean delivery of a baby in distress.

① 99360

② 99360 + 99360

③ 99464

④ 99465

26. Physician performed complex repair of a 3.2 cm scalp laceration.

① 13120

② 13120 + 13122

③ 13121

④ 13132

27. A 65-year-old patient receives anesthesia for repair of inguinal hernia. The patient has controlled hypertension. Include physical status modifier with code.

① 00830-P1

② 00830-P2

③ 00832-P1

④ 00832-P2

28. The patient underwent several burr holes in his skull with evacuation of subdural hematoma.

① 61105

② 61140

③ 61154

④ 61156

29. A 5-year-old patient, status post eardrum rupture, undergoes tympanic membrane repair with patch.

   ① 69433

   ② 69610

   ③ 69620

   ④ 69631

30. The patient was scheduled to see his physician for his six-month checkup and to have lab work done two weeks before his appointment on the 15th. As directed, the lab work was done on the first of the month. The patient called the physician's office on the 3rd and talked to him for 15 minutes about the tests. The doctor ordered two more tests done by the 5th so that the findings would be in the office for the patient's appointment on the 15th. What code would be reported for the service on the 3rd of the month?

   ① 99441

   ② 99442

   ③ 99443

   ④ 99444

31. Anesthesia was administered to a patient for a gastric bypass procedure due to her morbid obesity. Include the physical status modifier with code.

   ① 00700-P3

   ② 00790-P2

   ③ 00790-P3

   ④ 00797-P3

32. Physician performed excision of inguinal hidradenitis with complex repair.

   ① 11450

   ② 11451

   ③ 11462

   ④ 11463

33. The patient was scheduled to undergo extensive internal and external hemorrhoidectomy with fistulectomy. Ten minutes prior to the start of the procedure, after anesthesia had been administered, she experienced a rapid decrease in heart rate, and the physician canceled the procedure. The physician would report which of the following codes?

   ① 46260 + 46261

   ② 46260-52

   ③ 46260-53

   ④ 46262-53

34. A 54-year-old male underwent cystourethroscopy and laser ablation of two bladder tumors, each approximately 2.7 cm in size.

   ① 52000 + 52214

   ② 52214

   ③ 52234

   ④ 52235

35. The surgeon performed an excision of Peyronie plaque with a 4.0 cm graft.

   ① 54060

   ② 54065

   ③ 54110

   ④ 54111

36. Hand specialist performs neuroplasty of the ulnar nerve of the left wrist.

   ① 64704-LT

   ② 64718-LT

   ③ 64719-LT

   ④ 64721-LT

37. A 15-year-old male patient is seen by his new doctor for a comprehensive physical examination and immunizations. He also has moderate acne on face and chest.

    ① 99384

    ② 99384-25

    ③ 99394

    ④ 99394-25

38. The patient had his right thumb replanted following a complete amputation from the distal tip to the MP joint.

    ① 20816

    ② 20822

    ③ 20824

    ④ 20827

39. The surgeon performed a laryngoscopy for removal of a chicken bone fragment.

    ① 31511

    ② 31530

    ③ 31531

    ④ 31577

40. The patient, who has a history of hypertriglyceridemia but with normal cholesterol, now has his triglyceride level determined.

    ① 82465

    ② 83705

    ③ 84478

    ④ 84485

41. A patient with asthma is evaluated for use of a nebulizer.

    ① 94640

    ② 94644

    ③ 94660

    ④ 94664

42. The physician performs an independent medical examination for a patient to determine Worker's Compensation impairment rating.

    ① 99450

    ② 99455

    ③ 99456

    ④ 99499

43. The patient receives anesthesia for extracorporeal shock-wave lithotripsy with water bath. He has mild asthma. Include the physical status modifier with code.

    ① 00872-P1

    ② 00872-P2

    ③ 00873-P1

    ④ 00873-P2

44. The surgeon performs a single-lung transplant with cardiopulmonary bypass employed during the procedure.

    ① 32851

    ② 32852

    ③ 32853

    ④ 32854

45. The patient has an intestinal intussusception and undergoes a reduction via laparotomy.

    ① 44005

    ② 44020

    ③ 44050

    ④ 44055

46. The surgeon performs gastric bypass procedure with small intestine reconstruction to limit absorption for a patient who is morbidly obese.

    ① 43842

    ② 43846

    ③ 43847

    ④ 43848

47. The patient was seen in an initial office orthopedic consultation for bilateral trochanteric bursitis; her visit was considered problem-focused only.

① 99201

② 99241

③ 99242

④ 99251

48. The surgeon repairs an abdominal aortic aneurysm caused by high-grade atherosclerosis.

① 35001

② 35081

③ 35082

④ 35091

49. The physician successfully performed resuscitation for an infant suffering cardiac distress during delivery.

① 99461

② 99463

③ 99464

④ 99465

50. The patient underwent excision of a 1.5 cm malignant skin lesion of the left calf.

① 11402

② 11602

③ 11622

④ 11642

51. The patient returned to the office for a trigger point injection involving the trapezius and latissimus muscle groups.

① 20551

② 20552

③ 64415

④ 64420

52. The surgeon performed a hepatic artery ligation with complex suture repair of a liver laceration from a motor vehicle accident.

① 47350

② 47360

③ 47361

④ 47362

53. The physician sees the inpatient for follow-up after a left hip replacement. The physician performed a problem-focused history and physical examination with moderate decision making.

① 99221

② 99223

③ 99231

④ 99232

54. Family practitioner performed excision of a lipoma of the right forearm, 1.5 cm in diameter, followed by a simple wound closure.

① 11402

② 11402 + 12001

③ 11422

④ 11422 + 12031

55. Donor undergoes bone marrow harvesting for allogenic transplantation.

① 38220

② 38230

③ 38240

④ 38241

56. Patient has a total gastrectomy with Roux-en-Y reconstruction for stomach carcinoma.

① 43620

② 43621

③ 43631

④ 43633

57. Surgeon performed a simple Burch urethropexy on a 45-year-old patient.

① 51800

② 51840

③ 51841

④ 51992

58. A newly diagnosed patient with testicular cancer underwent radical orchiectomy with abdominal exploration via inguinal approach.

① 54520

② 54522

③ 54530

④ 54535

59. The patient had a reconstruction of the mandibular rami due to blunt trauma, undergoing C osteotomy with bone graft.

① 21188

② 21193

③ 21194

④ 21195

60. In the hospital radiology department, a bilateral lymphangiography of the lower extremities was performed.

① 75801

② 75803

③ 75805

④ 75807

61. The patient was seen on an initial, comprehensive endocrinology office visit, having been referred for signs and symptoms of new-onset diabetes.

① 99201

② 99204

③ 99212

④ 99214

62. The physician performs an emergency laparoscopic appendectomy.

① 44950

② 44960

③ 44970

④ 44979

63. The patient underwent nephrolithotomy for removal of a large staghorn calculus occupying the renal pelvis and calyces.

① 50060

② 50065

③ 50075

④ 50081

64. The surgeon performs a colonoscopy with removal of three polyps using hot biopsy forceps.

① 45333

② 45346

③ 45384

④ 45388

65. The physician conducts a home visit for a nonambulatory patient with progressive multiple sclerosis, now experiencing respiratory difficulty. The physician spent a total of 45 minutes with the new patient and family discussing treatment options and possible admission to a nursing facility. The physician performed a detailed history and exam with decision making of moderate complexity.

① 99342

② 99343

③ 99348

④ 99349

66. The surgeon performed a thoracotomy for a wedge biopsy of left lung mass.

① 32096

② 32097

③ 32035

④ 32551

67. The patient underwent marsupialization of a Bartholin gland cyst.

    ① 10040

    ② 10060

    ③ 56420

    ④ 56440

68. The patient seen in the outpatient physical therapy department received 15 minutes of ultrasound therapy on the left hip for bursitis.

    ① 97033

    ② 97035

    ③ 97110

    ④ 97124

69. The patient is seen for lipid panel study, including total serum cholesterol, HDL, and triglycerides.

    ① 82465 + 83718 + 84478

    ② 80061

    ③ 80076

    ④ 82705

70. The patient underwent pericardial window creation for drainage of excess pericardial fluid.

    ① 33010

    ② 33015

    ③ 33020

    ④ 33025

71. The patient has a simple papilloma of the penis and underwent cryosurgical removal.

    ① 54056

    ② 54057

    ③ 54065

    ④ 54110

72. A physician, who specializes in pain management, performs single lumbar epidural steroid injection.

    ① 62280

    ② 62282

    ③ 62311

    ④ 62319

73. The patient had an emergency head CT scan without contrast following blunt trauma to the skull.

    ① 70450

    ② 70470

    ③ 70496

    ④ 70540

74. Nuclear medicine ventilation and perfusion lung scan was performed on a patient with sudden shortness of breath; aerosol technique was used, and two projections were obtained.

    ① 78579

    ② 78580

    ③ 78582

    ④ 78598

75. The patient was treated with femoral-popliteal venous bypass grafting for severe occlusive disease.

    ① 35450

    ② 35521

    ③ 35556

    ④ 35566

76. A 12-year-old patient underwent dilation of the urethra under general anesthesia.

    ① 53605

    ② 53660

    ③ 53661

    ④ 53665

77. The surgeon performed a radial keratotomy procedure in the right eye.

    ① 65710-RT

    ② 65760-RT

    ③ 65767-RT

    ④ 65771-RT

78. Combative patient underwent removal of burrowed insect from external auditory canal; general anesthesia was required.

    ① 69145

    ② 69200

    ③ 69205

    ④ 69220

79. A 29-year-old pregnant female with twins, in her second trimester, underwent obstetrical ultrasound with detailed fetal anatomic exam.

    ① 76805 + 76810

    ② 76811 + 76812

    ③ 76815

    ④ 76856

80. The lab performs a test to determine the therapeutic level for a patient taking lithium.

    ① 80332

    ② 80338

    ③ 80375

    ④ 80178

81. A steelworker was seen in the emergency room for acute eye pain associated with a probable steel shaving in the eye; none was found. The physician performed a problem-focused history and physician examination with straightforward decision making.

    ① 99281

    ② 99283

    ③ 99284

    ④ 99285

82. The surgeon performs a closure of a rectovaginal fistula by vaginal approach.

    ① 57284

    ② 57300

    ③ 57305

    ④ 57310

83. The patient underwent MRI studies of the pelvis, first without contrast followed by use of contrast.

    ① 72191

    ② 72193

    ③ 72197

    ④ 72198

84. The surgeon performed an open repair of a femoral neck fracture with internal fixation.

    ① 27230

    ② 27235

    ③ 27236

    ④ 27244

85. The patient underwent tubal occlusion with the use of Falope rings, vaginal approach.

    ① 58600

    ② 58615

    ③ 58671

    ④ 58700

86. The physician replaces the permanent pacemaker pulse generator with a new model and attaches the previously placed dual leads.

    ① 33217

    ② 33228

    ③ 33241

    ④ 33263

87. The patient undergoes a sex-change operation from male to female.

① 55899

② 55970

③ 55980

④ 58999

88. The pregnant patient was visiting out-of-town family members when she went into labor. She returned home after the vaginal delivery. The physician that delivers the infant would report which of the following codes?

① 59400

② 59409

③ 59610

④ 59620

89. The patient underwent a right cataract extraction with the insertion of an intraocular lens via phacoemulsification technique.

① 66830

② 66850

③ 66982

④ 66984

90. The CPT Category III codes are updated quarterly.

① True

② False

91. The doctor orders a urinalysis to screen for bacteria.

① 81000

② 81002

③ 81003

④ 81007

92. The lab performed an automated CBC, WBC, and platelet count.

① 85025

② 85027

③ 85041

④ 85048

93. The physician orders a test for total hepatitis A antibodies.

① 86706

② 86707

③ 86708

④ 86709

94. The patient underwent debridement with dressing for a small epidermal burn of the forearm in the physician's office.

① 16000

② 16020

③ 16025

④ 16030

95. The patient underwent magnetic resonance imaging of the chest, with contrast studies, to rule out a mass.

① 71550

② 71551

③ 71552

④ 71555

96. The orthopedic surgeon performed a closed manipulation of her distal fibular fracture.

① 27781

② 27786

③ 27788

④ 27792

97. The surgeon performs a laparoscopic-assisted vaginal hysterectomy (uterus 240 g) with bilateral salpingo-oophorectomy.

① 58260 + 58720

② 58262

③ 58552

④ 58552 + 58720

98. The patient is hospitalized for a mobilization rearrangement repair of a conjunctival laceration.

   ① 65270

   ② 65272

   ③ 65273

   ④ 65285

99. The operative note states that the patient underwent an excision of a lesion of the mucosa and underlying muscle of the vestibule of the mouth.

   ① 40812

   ② 40814

   ③ 40816

   ④ 40820

100. The surgeon performed a biopsy of the left breast, using a localization wire, under ultrasound guidance.

   ① 19081

   ② 19083

   ③ 19085

   ④ 19125

Current Procedural Terminology ©2014 American Medical Association. All Rights Reserved.

Name _____

Answer Sheet for Exam Questions: CPT

1. ① ② ③ ④
2. ① ② ③ ④
3. ① ② ③ ④
4. ① ② ③ ④
5. ① ② ③ ④
6. ① ② ③ ④
7. ① ② ③ ④
8. ① ② ③ ④
9. ① ② ③ ④
10. ① ② ③ ④
11. ① ② ③ ④
12. ① ② ③ ④
13. ① ② ③ ④
14. ① ② ③ ④
15. ① ② ③ ④
16. ① ② ③ ④
17. ① ② ③ ④
18. ① ② ③ ④
19. ① ② ③ ④
20. ① ② ③ ④
21. ① ② ③ ④
22. ① ② ③ ④
23. ① ② ③ ④
24. ① ② ③ ④
25. ① ② ③ ④
26. ① ② ③ ④
27. ① ② ③ ④
28. ① ② ③ ④
29. ① ② ③ ④

30. ① ② ③ ④
31. ① ② ③ ④
32. ① ② ③ ④
33. ① ② ③ ④
34. ① ② ③ ④
35. ① ② ③ ④
36. ① ② ③ ④
37. ① ② ③ ④
38. ① ② ③ ④
39. ① ② ③ ④
40. ① ② ③ ④
41. ① ② ③ ④
42. ① ② ③ ④
43. ① ② ③ ④
44. ① ② ③ ④
45. ① ② ③ ④
46. ① ② ③ ④
47. ① ② ③ ④
48. ① ② ③ ④
49. ① ② ③ ④
50. ① ② ③ ④
51. ① ② ③ ④
52. ① ② ③ ④
53. ① ② ③ ④
54. ① ② ③ ④
55. ① ② ③ ④
56. ① ② ③ ④
57. ① ② ③ ④
58. ① ② ③ ④

59. ① ② ③ ④
60. ① ② ③ ④
61. ① ② ③ ④
62. ① ② ③ ④
63. ① ② ③ ④
64. ① ② ③ ④
65. ① ② ③ ④
66. ① ② ③ ④
67. ① ② ③ ④
68. ① ② ③ ④
69. ① ② ③ ④
70. ① ② ③ ④
71. ① ② ③ ④
72. ① ② ③ ④
73. ① ② ③ ④
74. ① ② ③ ④
75. ① ② ③ ④
76. ① ② ③ ④
77. ① ② ③ ④
78. ① ② ③ ④
79. ① ② ③ ④
80. ① ② ③ ④
81. ① ② ③ ④
82. ① ② ③ ④
83. ① ② ③ ④
84. ① ② ③ ④
85. ① ② ③ ④
86. ① ② ③ ④
87. ① ② ③ ④

88. ① ② ③ ④
89. ① ② ③ ④
90. ① ②
91. ① ② ③ ④
92. ① ② ③ ④
93. ① ② ③ ④
94. ① ② ③ ④
95. ① ② ③ ④
96. ① ② ③ ④
97. ① ② ③ ④
98. ① ② ③ ④
99. ① ② ③ ④
100. ① ② ③ ④

Name _____

Exam Questions for CPT and HCPCS

Directions: Use the appropriate coding manual to determine the correct choice for each situation.

1. To report ambulance services for a Medicare patient ordered by a physician, use modifier:

   ① -QM

   ② -QN

   ③ -QP

   ④ -SC

2. The patient underwent simple incision and drainage of an abscess on his thigh. The wound was packed with iodoform sterile gauze (approximately 2 inches × 2 inches). Select the correct codes for the procedure and the gauze.

   ① 10060 + A6220

   ② 10060 + A6222

   ③ 10061 + A6222

   ④ 10061 + A6223

3. HCPCS Level II codes are four character alphanumeric codes used to represent items not included in Level I (CPT) codes.

   ① True

   ② False

4. The patient undergoes an IVP but has a severe reaction to the contrast material. The IVP procedure is discontinued. Which modifier is used to describe this situation?

   ① -22

   ② -52

   ③ -53

   ④ -56

5. A 82-year-old patient was seen in the urgent care center with signs and symptoms of dehydration. She was observed for 8 hours while receiving IV normal saline infusion, 1000 cc. Select the correct HCPCS code for the infusion.

   ① J7030

   ② J7040

   ③ J7050

   ④ J7120

6. The L group of codes represents which procedures or products?

   ① Pathology and laboratory

   ② Drugs and enterals

   ③ Orthotics and prosthetics

   ④ Speech and language services

7. In CPT coding, the history, examination, and medical decision making are considered the key components in selecting the level of E/M services.

   ① True

   ② False

8. If a patient has trigger thumb release performed on the right, which modifier is used for the anatomic location?

   ① -F4

   ② -F5

   ③ -F9

   ④ -FA

9. A nursing facility patient developed multiple decubitus ulcers during a hospital stay. Her physician readmitted her to the nursing facility, performed a detailed history and exam, developed a new plan of care, and ordered an air-fluidized bed for treatment. Select the correct E/M and HCPCS codes.

① 99304 + E0193

② 99304 + E0194

③ 99305 + E0193

④ 99305 + E0194

10. HCPCS Level II codes are maintained by the American Medical Association.

① True

② False

11. A patient was seen in consultation for possible surgery. The surgeon schedules the procedure for the following day. Which modifier would you choose to indicate the decision for surgery?

① -54

① -55

③ -56

④ -57

12. Select the correct HCPCS code for an insertion tray (use of accessories only) without drainage bag or catheter.

① A4310

② A4311

③ A4312

④ A4313

13. Select the correct HCPCS code for below-knee-length surgical stockings.

① A4490

② A4495

③ A4500

④ A4510

14. According to CPT definitions, a patient treated in an ambulatory facility would be classified as an outpatient.

① True

② False

15. The patient has incision and drainage of an abscess involving the left fourth toe. Identify the correct modifier.

① -T2

② -T3

③ -T6

④ -T8

16. A 50-year-old female was seen in the office for a facial chemical peel, epidermal only.

① 15780

② 15786

③ 15788

④ 15789

17. H codes in HCPCS represent the official codes for durable medical equipment.

① True

② False

18. The patient arrived in the emergency department with acute shortness of breath. During his observation in the emergency department, multiple arterial blood gas testing was performed to monitor his improvement. Which modifier would you choose to accurately code the multiple ABGs?

① -51

② -90

③ -91

④ -99

19. Select the correct HCPCS code for a tourniquet used by a dialysis patient.

    ① A4911

    ② A4913

    ③ A4918

    ④ A4929

20. Select the correct HCPCS code for a pair of aluminum underarm crutches.

    ① E0110

    ② E0112

    ③ E0114

    ④ E0116

21. Physical status modifiers in CPT are used to distinguish the varying levels of complexity of surgical services provided.

    ① True

    ② False

22. A patient with Medicare insurance received a wheelchair two months ago, but the beneficiary has not decided whether to purchase or rent. Which HCPCS modifier would you use?

    ① -BO

    ② -BP

    ③ -BR

    ④ -BU

23. A teenager, new to the practice, was seen in a problem-focused visit for symptoms of tonsillitis and pharyngitis. She was given an injection of azithromycin for her acute symptoms. Select the correct E/M and HCPCS codes.

    ① 99201 + J0290

    ② 99201 + J0456

    ③ 99202 + J0290

    ④ 99202 + J0456

24. It is acceptable to code HCPCS from index entries only.

    ① True

    ② False

25. A 31-year-old patient was seen by her family doctor for a routine physical exam. During the exam, the patient was noted to have high blood pressure. The physician discussed the new finding with the patient, and the patient disclosed she has been under a great deal of stress due to the demands of her work and impending divorce. The high blood pressure was deemed stress-related, and the physician and the patient discussed stress reduction techniques. As a result of the extended discussion with the patient, the visit was prolonged 35 minutes beyond the normally expected length for a routine physical exam. Which CPT code(s) or modifier(s) would you use to document the additional time spent with the patient?

    ① 99395-P3

    ② 99395-22

    ③ 99395 + 99354

    ④ 99358

26. Select the correct HCPCS code for a surgically implanted electrical osteogenesis stimulator.

    ① E0748

    ② E0749

    ③ E0760

    ④ E0761

27. Select the correct HCPCS code to report a patient receiving an injection of amphotericin B, 50 mg.

    ① J0285

    ② J0287 x 5

    ③ J0288 x 5

    ④ J0289 x 5

28. The general definition of the CPT surgical package includes the patient's preoperative evaluation on the day of the procedure, the surgical procedure and its usual components, and the patient's uncomplicated follow-up care.

① True

② False

29. The patient had a skin tag removed from her upper right eyelid. Which HCPCS modifier identifies this location?

① -E1

② -E2

③ -E3

④ -E4

30. An infant born with clubfoot on the right was seen in the pediatric orthopedic clinic as a new patient. The physician conducted a problem-focused history and examination and prescribed a clubfoot wedge for the patient. Select the correct codes for the visit and the wedge.

① 99201 + L3201

② 99201 + L3380

③ 99212 + L3201

④ 99212 + L3380

31. The HCPCS route of administration "JA" means the patient is receiving the drug intravenously.

① True

② False

32. The patient was seen in the office for exercise stress testing. When the physician was placing the EKG leads, she noticed a suspicious mole on the patient's chest and excised the lesion. What CPT modifier would you use to indicate the additional procedure performed during this E/M visit?

① -24

② -25

③ -51

④ -53

33. A patient was seen in the office for acute hives. The doctor gave her a 25 mg injection of hydroxyzine. Select the correct HCPCS code.

① J3400

② J3410

③ J3470

④ J3485

34. Select the correct HCPCS code for an orthopedic shoe insole made of felt and covered with leather.

① L3500

② L3520

③ L3540

④ L3570

35. To measure and code the removal of a lesion using CPT guidelines, the lesion size must be expressed in inches.

① True

② False

36. If a patient is prescribed oxygen therapy at 0.5 liters per minute, which HCPCS modifier describes this flow rate?

① -QE

② -QF

③ -QG

④ -QH

37. An established patient was seen in the office because of difficulty toileting after hip replacement surgery. Her family doctor examined her and sent her home with a stationary commode chair with fixed arms to use during her recovery period. The physician performed a problem-focused history and physical exam with straightforward decision making. Select the appropriate codes.

① 99211 + E0163

② 99211 + E0165

③ 99212 + E0163

④ 99212 + E0165

38. All HCPCS codes and descriptions are updated monthly by CMS.

    ① True

    ② False

39. Which CPT modifier would you choose to indicate a patient received a service or procedure that was less than originally intended?

    ① -22

    ② -32

    ③ -51

    ④ -52

40. Select the correct HCPCS code that describes the reduction of an ocular prosthesis.

    ① V2623

    ② V2625

    ③ V2626

    ④ V2629

41. The patient received an intramuscular injection of 2 mg of Haloperidol in the physician's office. Select the correct HCPCS code.

    ① J1630

    ② J1631

    ③ J3410

    ④ J3470

42. When coding bilateral procedures in CPT, you must always list the code twice.

    ① True

    ② False

43. The mobile x-ray service came to the nursing facility to x-ray a resident for possible hip fracture. The x-ray will be interpreted tomorrow by the radiologist. Which HCPCS modifier would you use for today's service?

    ① -TA

    ② -TC

    ③ -TD

    ④ -TE

44. A Medicare patient with diabetes saw the doctor for routine foot care: the cutting of three calluses and debridement of all 10 toenails.

    ① 11056 + 11719

    ② 11056 + 11721

    ③ 11057 + 11720

    ④ S0390

45. Laboratory services in HCPCS are listed in the P codes grouping.

    ① True

    ② False

46. Which CPT modifier would you use to indicate that an outside laboratory was used to process a patient's specimen?

    ① -56

    ② -90

    ③ -91

    ④ -99

47. Select the correct HCPCS code for a patient receiving nonemergency minibus transportation in a mountain area.

    ① A0080

    ② A0110

    ③ A0120

    ④ A0160

48. Some radiology procedures include two parts: a technical component and a professional component.

    ① True

    ② False

49. A patient has used his wheelchair for nearly four years. Due to wear, he now needs a replacement for the right footrest. Which HCPCS modifier is used to indicate this replacement?

① -RA

② -RB

③ -RR

④ -RT

50. The patient was referred to the office of a wound care specialist for consultation regarding his nonhealing surgical wound. The physician spent approximately 30 minutes and performed an expanded problem-focused history and examination with straightforward decision making. The patient was sent home on a topical hyperbaric oxygen chamber therapy for wound healing. Select the correct codes.

① 99241 + A4575

② 99242 + A4575

③ 99251 + A4575

④ 99252 + A4575

51. Drugs listed in HCPCS are identified by both brand and generic names.

① True

② False

52. The patient had an emergency cholecystectomy six days after having a lung biopsy. The same surgeon performed both procedures. Which CPT modifier is used on the second surgery?

① -58

② -59

③ -78

④ -79

53. What is the correct HCPCS code for a patient that requires gradient compression stockings, full length 30–40 mmHg?

① A6531

② A6534 x 2

③ A6537 x 2

④ A6540

54. A 72-year-old female patient was seen for insertion of a temporary, indwelling latex Foley urinary catheter. Select the correct codes.

① 51701 + A4314

② 51701 + A4338

③ 51702 + A4338

④ 51703 + A4328

55. According to CPT coding guidelines, a pathology consultation includes a medical interpretive report.

① True

② False

56. The physician amputated the patient's right lower extremity (BKA). His staff physician assistant (PA) was assisting during the procedure. Which HCPCS modifier would you choose to indicate the PA's role in this procedure?

① -AD

② -AM

③ -AS

④ -AT

57. The nurse saw the patient for a routine visit in the multiple sclerosis clinic. He received an injection of beta-1a interferon, 30 mcg, from the nurse in the clinic. Select the appropriate codes.

① 99211 + J1826

② 99211 + J9212

③ 99212 + J1826

④ 99212 + J9214

58. HCPCS ambulance modifiers always include one alpha character and one numeric character.

① True

② False

59. Anesthesia is administered, and the surgeon inserted the scope and begins to perform the planned diagnostic flexible fiberoptic laryngoscopy. Due to equipment failure, the procedure could not be accomplished. Which of the following would be used to report the physician's services?

① 31505-52

② 31525-52

③ 31525-53

④ 31575-53

60. Select the correct HCPCS code for a drainable rubber ostomy pouch with a faceplate attached.

① A4375

② A4376

③ A4377

④ A4378

61. Select the correct HCPCS code for replacement handgrip for a cane that the patient owns.

① A4635

② A4636

③ A4637

④ A4640

62. In CPT coding, when the patient receives an immune globulin product, you must also include an administration code as appropriate.

① True

② False

63. An ambulance was called to come to the aid of a choking patient; however, the patient expired before the ambulance arrived on the scene. Which HCPCS modifier would you use to document this circumstance?

① -QK

② -QL

③ -QM

④ -QP

64. The patient underwent unattended sleep study with monitoring of oxygen saturation, respiratory airflow, and heart rate. He was not able to sleep adequately throughout the study, and the study was equivocal. He was provided with a recording apnea monitor for home use. Select the appropriate codes.

① 95806 + E0618

② 95806 + E0619

③ 95807 + E0618

④ 95807 + E0619

65. The two levels of national HCPCS codes can be applied to both inpatient and outpatient services by physicians.

① True

② False

66. Which CPT modifier is used to indicate a repeat procedure performed by a different physician?

① -58

② -76

③ -77

④ -78

67. Select the correct HCPCS code for a hydrogel dressing with an adhesive border used to cover a 24-square inch wound.

① A6242

② A6244

③ A6246

④ A6247

68. Select the correct HCPCS code for home mix parenteral nutritional additives, to include electrolytes.

① B4197

② B4199

③ B4216

④ B4220

69. When coding in CPT, no distinction is made between new and established patients in the emergency department.

    ① True

    ② False

70. The patient was seen in the contraceptive clinic two weeks after delivery of her child. She was fitted with a copper intrauterine device. Select the codes for the fitting and the device.

    ① 58300 + J7303

    ② 58300 + J7300

    ③ 58301 + J7303

    ④ 58301 + J7300

71. Select the correct HCPCS code for a replacement brake attachment on a wheeled walker.

    ① E0143

    ② E0147

    ③ E0155

    ④ E0159

72. Select the correct HCPCS code for a patient admitted as an inpatient to a residential addiction program for acute alcohol detoxification.

    ① H0009

    ② H0011

    ③ H0012

    ④ H0013

73. The patient received a two-lead TENS unit for pain control after suffering a fractured radius. Select appropriate codes.

    ① 64550 + E0720

    ② 64550 + E0730

    ③ 64575 + E0720

    ④ 64575 + E0730

74. Select the correct HCPCS code for an injection of methylprednisolone acetate, 40 mg.

    ① J1020 x 2

    ② J1030

    ③ J1040

    ④ J2920

75. A patient came to the office to have a B12 level analysis and to receive her weekly B12 shot. Select the correct codes.

    ① 82607 + J3420

    ② 82607 + J3430

    ③ 82608 + J3420

    ④ 82608 + J3430

76. Select the HCPCS code that correctly identifies a unit of leukocyte-reduced platelets.

    ① P9019

    ② P9020

    ③ P9031

    ④ P9034

77. Select the correct HCPCS code for 1 mg of inhaled dexamethasone in concentrated form.

    ① J1094

    ② J1100

    ③ J7637

    ④ J7638

78. A patient who is status post left-sided CVA (cerebrovascular accident) was seen for weight loss and other symptoms indicative of dysphagia. Speech pathology provides dysphagia screening and her first treatment for the swallowing dysfunction. Select the correct codes.

    ① 92526 + V5362

    ② 92526 + V5364

    ③ 92610 + V5362

    ④ 92610 + V5364

79. Select the correct HCPCS code for a nonheated humidifier used with a positive airway pressure device.

① A7039

② E0550

③ E0560

④ E0561

80. The physician spent 30 minutes with the patient and family to discuss discharge plans on the day of discharge as well as the patient's immediate at-home care. The patient had undergone his second below-knee amputation and was given a transfer board for use at home. Select the codes for the discharge visit and the transfer board.

① 99238 + E0705

② 99238 + E1035

③ 99239 + E0705

④ 99239 + E1035

81. Select the correct HCPCS code that reflects the supply of a one-dose vial of technetium Tc 99m disofenin.

① A9500

② A9502

③ A9510

④ A9536

82. Identify the HCPCS code that describes a full-leg, segmental pneumatic appliance with compressor.

① E0650

② E0660

③ E0667

④ E0671

83. Select the HCPCS code for an injection of 2 grams of cefotaxime sodium.

① J0694 x2

② J0696

③ J0697

④ J0698 x 2

84. What is the correct HCPCS modifier that is reported for an outpatient diabetes management training group for a 60-minute session?

① G0108

② G0108 × 2

③ G0109

④ G0109 × 2

85. The patient was prepped and anesthesia was administered for the planned esophagogastro-duodenoscopy (EGD) performed in the hospital outpatient surgery center. The flexible scope was inserted transorally. Due to equipment failure, the endoscopic exam could not be completed. What CPT code and HCPCS modifier would be used to report the services on the hospital claim form?

① 43200-53

② 43200-74

③ 43235-53

④ 43235-74

86. At the physician's direction, the RN called the patient at home to monitor the patient's program for control of her severe arthritis.

① S0220

② S0271

③ S0315

④ S0320

87. The patient was fitted with a custom-made compression burn garment jacket for severe burns of the chest and upper back.

① A6501

② A6509

③ A6510

④ A6511

88. A patient with a fractured femur and tibia had a trapeze and grab bar attached to a hospital bed in his home.

① E0910

② E0920

③ E0940

④ E0941

89. Five patients participated in a 45-minute group psychotherapy session and received free educational materials.

① 90834 + 99071

② 90846 + 99070

③ 90853 + 99071

④ 90901 + 99070

90. A patient received a Blom Singer speech valve.

① L8499

② L8500

③ L8501

④ L8507

91. The patient received a replacement for a lost gas-permeable bifocal contact lens.

① V2430

② V2502

③ V2512

④ V2522

92. What HCPCS code would be reported for a bilateral digital screening mammography?

① G0202

② G0202 x 2

③ G0204

④ G0206

93. What HCPCS code is used to report a one unit of Enteral formula (nutritionally complete and customized composition) administered through a feeding tube?

① B4150

② B4152

③ B4153

④ B4154

94. A physician serves a large rural area, and some patients request their E/M services via the Internet. These documented encounters would be reported with code:

① 99056

② 99347

③ 99441

④ 99444

95. The infant with a left clubfoot was treated by manipulation and a short leg cast.

① 29405-LT

② 29425-LT

③ 29450-LT

④ 29799-LT

96. The patient's mother and sister have known BRCA1 mutation, and she now undergoes testing for the mutation.

① 81206

② 81210

③ 81214

④ 81216

97. A store specializing in shoes for diabetic patients supplied a patient with a pair that had a metatarsal bar.

① A5500 x 2

② A5503 x 2

③ A5504 x 2

④ A5505 x 2

98. Following his hospitalization, the patient went home with cervical traction equipment that fits over a door.

① E0840

② E0850

③ E0860

④ E0870

99. The patient was authorized to receive a new 12-volt battery charger.

① L7360

② L7362

③ L7364

④ L7366

100. A patient received 1 g of Gammagard liquid immune globulin intravenously from the nurse in his doctor's office, 45 minutes.

① 90281 + J1460

② 90281 + J1559

③ 90471 + J1559

④ 96365 + J1569 x 2

Name _____

Answer Sheet for Exam Questions: CPT and HCPCS

1. ① ② ③ ④
2. ① ② ③ ④
3. ① ②
4. ① ② ③ ④
5. ① ② ③ ④
6. ① ② ③ ④
7. ① ②
8. ① ② ③ ④
9. ① ② ③ ④
10. ① ②
11. ① ② ③ ④
12. ① ② ③ ④
13. ① ② ③ ④
14. ① ②
15. ① ② ③ ④
16. ① ② ③ ④
17. ① ②
18. ① ② ③ ④
19. ① ② ③ ④
20. ① ② ③ ④
21. ① ②
22. ① ② ③ ④
23. ① ② ③ ④
24. ① ②
25. ① ② ③ ④
26. ① ② ③ ④
27. ① ② ③ ④
28. ① ②
29. ① ② ③ ④

30. ① ② ③ ④
31. ① ②
32. ① ② ③ ④
33. ① ② ③ ④
34. ① ② ③ ④
35. ① ②
36. ① ② ③ ④
37. ① ② ③ ④
38. ① ②
39. ① ② ③ ④
40. ① ② ③ ④
41. ① ② ③ ④
42. ① ②
43. ① ② ③ ④
44. ① ② ③ ④
45. ① ②
46. ① ② ③ ④
47. ① ② ③ ④
48. ① ②
49. ① ② ③ ④
50. ① ② ③ ④
51. ① ②
52. ① ② ③ ④
53. ① ② ③ ④
54. ① ② ③ ④
55. ① ②
56. ① ② ③ ④
57. ① ② ③ ④
58. ① ②

59. ① ② ③ ④
60. ① ② ③ ④
61. ① ② ③ ④
62. ① ②
63. ① ② ③ ④
64. ① ② ③ ④
65. ① ②
66. ① ② ③ ④
67. ① ② ③ ④
68. ① ② ③ ④
69. ① ②
70. ① ② ③ ④
71. ① ② ③ ④
72. ① ② ③ ④
73. ① ② ③ ④
74. ① ② ③ ④
75. ① ② ③ ④
76. ① ② ③ ④
77. ① ② ③ ④
78. ① ② ③ ④
79. ① ② ③ ④
80. ① ② ③ ④
81. ① ② ③ ④
82. ① ② ③ ④
83. ① ② ③ ④
84. ① ② ③ ④
85. ① ② ③ ④
86. ① ② ③ ④
87. ① ② ③ ④

88. ① ② ③ ④
89. ① ② ③ ④
90. ① ② ③ ④
91. ① ② ③ ④
92. ① ② ③ ④
93. ① ② ③ ④
94. ① ② ③ ④
95. ① ② ③ ④
96. ① ② ③ ④
97. ① ② ③ ④
98. ① ② ③ ④
99. ① ② ③ ④
100. ① ② ③ ④

Name _____

Exam Questions for ICD-10-CM

Directions: Use the appropriate coding manual to determine the correct choice for each situation.

1. A patient seen in the office today has known Graves' disease, now seen with thyrotoxic storm.

   ① E05.01

   ② E05.20

   ③ E05.90

   ④ E05.91

2. A 3-year-old patient was brought into the office by her mother because of fever, fussiness, and tugging at the right ear. Otoscopy confirmed acute infection with erythema and pus of the canal.

   ① H65.191

   ② H65.194

   ③ H66.001

   ④ H66.002

3. A patient was seen because of pain and swelling of the right elbow. The joint does not appear to be unstable, but there is effusion. Ruled out fracture.

   ① M25.421

   ② M25.521

   ③ S42.391A

   ④ A42.401A

4. The patient took the ampicillin as directed but returns to the office today with urticaria and swelling, classic signs of allergic reaction.

   ① L50.0, T36.0x5A

   ② L50.8

   ③ L50.0, T36.0x4A

   ④ T88.6

5. Newly diagnosed asthma patient was counseled regarding asthma therapy and the correct use of a nebulizer. What is the correct code for counselling?

   ① Z71.89

   ② Z71.9

   ③ Z97.8

   ④ Z99.89

6. The patient is brought to the physician's office for red sores. The physician documents the diagnosis as impetigo.

   ① L01.00

   ② L01.01

   ③ L01.09

   ④ R21

7. The patient was seen for evaluation of pilonidal cyst.

   ① L05.01

   ② L05.02

   ③ L05.91

   ④ L05.92

8. A 34-year-old male came to the office for examination of a penile lesion; his physician determined it to be a classic plaque of Peyronie's disease.

   ① N47.8

   ② N48.0

   ③ N48.6

   ④ N48.29

9. The patient was seen for annual gynecological exam including Pap smear. Findings were normal.

   ① Z01.411, Z12.4

   ② Z01.411, Z12.72

   ③ Z01.419, Z12.4

   ④ Z01.419, Z12.72

10. Visit regarding patient needing a refill for her birth-control pills.

   ① Z30.40

   ② Z30.41

   ③ Z30.431

   ④ Z30.49

11. The patient suffered a dislocation of the left shoulder.

   ① S43.001A

   ② S43.004A

   ③ S43.005A

   ④ S43.006A

12. Select the correct code for a unilateral strangulated inguinal hernia.

   ① K40.30

   ② K40.31

   ③ K40.90

   ④ K40.91

13. A 24-year-old female patient was seen for vaginal spotting in her 21st week of pregnancy.

   ① O26.851, Z3A.21

   ② O26.852, Z3A.21

   ③ O26.853, Z3A.21

   ④ O26.859, Z3A.21

14. A 35-year-old female was seen in the office today for evaluation of a breast lump.

   ① N61

   ② N62

   ③ N63

   ④ N64.5

15. A 16-year-old male was seen in the clinic for severe sore throat, redness, cough, and erythema. Rapid strep test was positive. The diagnosis is documented as Streptococcal pharyngitis.

   ① J02.0

   ② J02.8

   ③ J02.8, B95.5

   ④ J02.9

16. Select the correct code for personal history of cervical carcinoma.

   ① C53.9

   ② Z80.49

   ③ Z85.41

   ④ Z85.44

17. The patient was seen for treatment of acute posttraumatic stress disorder.

   ① F43.0

   ② F43.10

   ③ F43.11

   ④ F43.12

18. The patient was diagnosed with a chronic gastric ulcer with bleeding.

   ① K25.0

   ② K25.3

   ③ K25.4

   ④ K25.6

19. The physician documents the following diagnosis: alcoholic hepatitis with alcohol dependence and withdrawal delirium.

   ① F10.231, K70.10

   ② F10.239, K70.10

   ③ F10.230, K70.11

   ④ F10.231, K70.11

20. The patient was seen for a puncture wound of the right forearm.

① S41.131A

② S51.811A

③ S51.831A

④ S51.841A

21. A patient came to the office to discuss treatment options for a new diagnosis of malignant melanoma of the forehead.

① C43.30

② C43.39

③ C43.9

④ C44.309

22. A 10-year-old patient was brought in for evaluation of skin tags of the neck.

① L91.0

② L91.8

③ L91.9

④ L98.9

23. A patient's daughter brought her father in for follow-up of early-onset Alzheimer's dementia.

① G30.0, F02.80

② G30.0, F02.81

③ G30.8, F02.80

④ G30.9, F02.80

24. A patient was brought into the office for evaluation and examination after swallowing a dime.

① T17.208A

② T18.2xxA

③ T18.8xxA

④ T18.9xxA

25. A vacationing patient was seen in the urgent care clinic for second-degree sunburn of both shoulder areas.

① L55.0

② L55.1

③ L55.9

④ T22.251A, T22.252A

26. Select the correct code for chlamydial conjunctivitis.

① A74.0

② A74.89

③ A74.0, H10.9

④ H10.9

27. The patient was seen in the office seeking treatment for a fungal toenail infection.

① B35.1

② L03.032

③ L08.9

④ L08.9, B49

28. A patient was seen in the office today for a routine follow-up after suffering a comminuted fracture of the shaft of the left femur. Physician notes that the fracture is healing.

① S72.352A

② S72.352D

③ S72.355A

④ S72.355D

29. The patient was seen for removal of a Jackson-Pratt drain inserted last week after cholecystectomy.

① Z48.02

② Z48.03

③ Z48.817

④ Z51.89

30. A 6-year-old child was brought in for additional testing for color blindness.

    ① H53.50
    ② H53.52
    ③ H53.59
    ④ H53.9

31. The patient was seen for complaints of increased urinary frequency due to benign prostatic hypertrophy.

    ① N40.0, R35.0
    ② N40.0
    ③ N40.1
    ④ N40.1, R35.0

32. Select the correct code(s) for malignant hypertensive heart disease with stage 3 chronic renal failure.

    ① I11.9, I12.9, N18.3
    ② I13.10, N18.9
    ③ I13.10, N18.3
    ④ I13.11, N18.3

33. A patient was seen for preoperative cardiovascular evaluation prior to undergoing cholecystectomy.

    ① Z01.810
    ② Z01.818
    ③ Z01.89
    ④ Z02.89

34. A 19-year-old male was seen in the emergency department for a nondisplaced fracture of the trapezoid, smaller multiangular, of the right wrist.

    ① S62.174A
    ② S62.175A
    ③ S62.181A
    ④ S62.184A

35. Select the correct code(s) for cellulitis of the colostomy site.

    ① K94.00
    ② K94.02, L03.311
    ③ N99.511
    ④ T85.698A, L03.311

36. Select the correct code for Charcôt's joint of the right knee.

    ① M14.651
    ② M14.661
    ③ M14.671
    ④ M14.669

37. A 52-year-old female was seen by the gastroenterologist for evaluation of prolapsed internal hemorrhoids and anal fissure.

    ① K64.1
    ② K64.8, K60.0
    ③ K64.8, K60.2
    ④ K64.9, K60.3

38. A patient was seen in the office for severe vertigo and loss of hearing. She was diagnosed with bilateral labyrinthitis.

    ① H83.03
    ② H83.2x3
    ③ H83.01, H83.02
    ④ H83.2x1, H83.2x2

39. Select the correct code(s) for idiopathic scoliosis of the cervicothoracic region.

    ① M41.23
    ② M41.83
    ③ M41.9
    ④ M41.22, M41.24

40. A 62-year-old male was evaluated for varicose veins with stasis dermatitis of the left lower extremity.

   ① I83.10

   ② I83.12

   ③ I83.028

   ④ I83.223

41. The patient was seen for continuing evaluation of Marfan's syndrome with dilation of the aorta.

   ① Q87.40

   ② Q87.43

   ③ Q87.410

   ④ Q87.418

42. A patient was seen for ongoing evaluation of pernicious anemia.

   ① D51.0

   ② D53.9

   ③ D63.8

   ④ D64.9

43. Select the correct code for Type II diabetes mellitus causing mononeuropathy.

   ① E10.41

   ② E11.40

   ③ E11.41

   ④ E11.42

44. A 55-year-old male was seen in a follow-up for a right bundle-branch block with left posterior fascicular bundle-branch block.

   ① I45.2

   ② I45.3

   ③ I45.4

   ④ I44.7, I45.19

45. Patient has sepsis due to a puncture wound of the lower back.

   ① A41.9, S31.030A

   ② A41.9, S31.031A

   ③ S31.041A, A41.9

   ④ A41.9, S31.040A

46. The patient is seen for ongoing treatment of Type II diabetes mellitus. The patient explains that she is not taking her medication (metformin) because she is unemployed and has no insurance.

   ① E10.9, T38.3x5A, Z91.128

   ② E10.9, T38.3x6A, Z91.120

   ③ E11.9, T38.3x5A, Z91.128

   ④ E11.9, T38.3x6A, Z91.120

47. A patient was seen for the chief complaint of losing her sense of smell after a bout of the flu.

   ① G96.9

   ② R43.0

   ③ R43.1

   ④ R43.8

48. A 42-year-old female was seen for treatment of situational depression due to impending divorce.

   ① F43.0

   ② F43.21

   ③ F43.22

   ④ F43.29

49. Select the correct code for acquired trigger finger, right index finger.

   ① M65.321

   ② M65.322

   ③ Q74.0

   ④ Q79.8

50. Select the correct code for spontaneous rupture of the Achilles tendon, right leg.

    ① M66.38

    ② M66.361

    ③ M66.369

    ④ M66.861

51. A 32-year-old pregnant female was seen for vaginal bleeding; placenta previa was detected. She is in the early second trimester of pregnancy.

    ① O44.00

    ② O44.02

    ③ O44.11

    ④ O44.12

52. Select the correct code for narcolepsy.

    ① G47.41

    ② G47.411

    ③ G47.419

    ④ G47.429

53. The patient had episodes of "zoning out" and, after extensive observation and testing, he was diagnosed with absence epileptic seizures.

    ① G40.A01

    ② G40.A09

    ③ G40.A11

    ④ G40.A19

54. The patient was found to have a severe allergy to dog hair.

    ① J30.1

    ② J30.2

    ③ J30.81

    ④ J30.89

55. A 23-year-old male was seen in the Emergency Department for treatment of mild frostbite of the right toes.

    ① T33.831A

    ② T33.832A

    ③ T33.839A

    ④ T34.831A

56. The patient received an accidental, self-inflicted laceration of the palm of his right hand while using a kitchen knife.

    ① S61.401A, W26.0xxA

    ② S61.411A, W26.0xxA

    ③ S61.411S, W26.0xxS

    ④ S61.421A, W26.0A

57. A 61-year-old male was seen in consultation for hydrocodone abuse.

    ① F11.10

    ② F11.120

    ③ F11.20

    ④ F19.10

58. Patient seen in the office for follow-up after suffering an acute myocardial infarction (ST elevation) of the anterior wall.

    ① I21.09

    ② I21.11

    ③ I22.0

    ④ I25.11

59. Select the correct code for acute upper respiratory infection with influenza.

    ① J10.1

    ② J10.1, J11.1

    ③ J11.1

    ④ J11.39

60. Select the correct codes for accidental poisoning with whiskey.

① T51.0x1A

② T51.0x4A

③ T51.0x4S

④ T51.91xA

61. The patient returns to the office for ongoing evaluation of dysphasia. He suffered a cerebrovascular accident (nontraumatic intracranial hemorrhage) 6 months ago.

① I69.221

② I62.9, R47.01

③ R47.01

④ S06.9x0S

62. Patient admitted to the hospital for choledocho-lithiasis with acute cholangitis and obstruction.

① K80.31

② K80.33

③ K80.35

④ K80.37

63. The patient was seen in the office for ongoing treatment of chronic gonococcal cystitis.

① A54.01

② A54.03

③ A54.23

④ N30.2

64. Full-term infant born in the hospital by vaginal delivery. Baby has fetal alcohol syndrome.

① Z38.00, O35.4

② Z38.00, Q86.0

③ Z38.1, O35.4

④ Z38.1, Q86.0

65. The patient presents for surgical removal of pilomatrixoma of the right helix region.

① C44.202

② D23.21

③ D23.22

④ D48.5

66. A 34-year-old male suffered a severe burn over one year ago and is being evaluated for continued mononeuropathy of the left thigh, secondary to the burn.

① G57.72, T24.012A

② G57.71, T24.032S

③ G57.92, T24.012S

④ G57.92, T24.032S

67. The patient was seen in the office for pain due to phantom limb syndrome.

① G54.4

② G54.6

③ G54.7

④ G54.9

68. Select the correct code for arteriovenous malformation of the right lower extremity requiring surgical treatment.

① Q26.8

② Q27.32

③ Q27.9

④ Q84.9

69. The patient is seen for ongoing treatment of diverticulitis of the large intestines.

① K57.30

② K57.31

③ K57.32

④ K57.33

70. A 52-year-old male is being treated in the hospital for severe mitral regurgitation.

   ① I05.8

   ② I05.9

   ③ I34.0

   ④ I34.8

71. An 83-year-old male was treated for pneumonia due to *Streptococcus pneumoniae*.

   ① J13

   ② J15.3

   ③ J15.4

   ④ J15.8

72. The patient seeks treatment in the emergency department. The diagnosis is documented as Type II open fracture of the medial condyle of the left tibia.

   ① S82.132A

   ② S82.132B

   ③ S82.135A

   ④ S82.135B

73. A 48-year-old male returns to the office for ongoing physical therapy to regain strength in his back after a thoracic ligament strain at work.

   ① S23.3xxD

   ② S23.3xxA, Z51.89

   ③ S23.3xxD, Z51.89

   ④ S23.8xxA

74. Select the correct code for mildly persistent asthma with acute exacerbation.

   ① J45.20

   ② J45.21

   ③ J45.31

   ④ J45.32

75. A patient was seen for evaluation and treatment of neurogenic bladder.

   ① N31.0

   ② N31.8

   ③ N31.9

   ④ N32.89

76. The patient presents to outpatient physical therapy after a left hip replacement for severe osteoarthritis.

   ① M16.12

   ② Z47.1, M16.12

   ③ Z47.1, Z96.642

   ④ Z47.89

77. A 53-year-old male was seen today for his weekly chemotherapy infusion following a recent diagnosis of carcinoma of the descending colon.

   ① Z51.11, C18.6

   ② Z51.11, C78.5

   ③ Z51.89, C18.6

   ④ Z51.89, C78.5

78. A 56-year-old male patient is being seen for severe recurrent major depression.

   ① F33.0

   ② F33.1

   ③ F33.2

   ④ F33.40

79. A patient presents to the physician's office with hot flashes and insomnia. The physician documents the diagnosis as premature menopause.

   ① E28.310

   ② E28.319

   ③ E28.310, R50.9, F51.01

   ④ R50.9, F51.01

80. The patient presents with a senile entropion of the right upper eyelid.

① H02.031

② H02.032

③ H02.034

① H02.001

81. Select the correct code for a hiatal hernia with obstruction.

① K44.0

② K44.1

③ K44.9

④ K45.0

82. The patient has Type II diabetes mellitus with foot ulcer, confined to the epidermis.

① E11.621, L97.421

② E11.621, L97.422

③ E11.622, L97.421

④ E11.622, L97.429

83. The patient is evaluated for sudden total blindness of the right eye; the left eye was not affected.

① H53.13

② H53.62

③ H54.41

④ H54.42

84. Select the correct code for emphysema with chronic obstructive bronchitis.

① J43.8, J44.1

② J43.8, J44.9

③ J44.1

④ J44.9

85. Adult male was diagnosed with whooping cough due to *Bordetella parapertussis*.

① A37.00

② A37.01

③ A37.10

④ A37.11

86. The patient was suffering from near-syncopal episodes and was diagnosed with an electrolyte imbalance.

① E87.0

② E87.3

③ E87.70

④ E87.8

87. A 34-year-old male is HIV positive and now has evidence of Kaposi lesions on the skin.

① B20

② B20, C46.0

③ C46.1, B20

④ B20, C46.1

88. The patient is in her third trimester of pregnancy and has gestational edema.

① O12.01

② O12.02

③ O12.03

④ O26.03

89. The patient was diagnosed with a left recurrent inguinal hernia with gangrene.

① K40.11

② K40.31

③ K40.41

④ K40.91

90. The patient is seeking initial treatment for a stress fracture of the left tibia.

① M84.361A

② M84.362A

③ M84.364A

④ S82.202A

91. Patient is admitted to the hospital with acute cholecystitis and obstruction of the gallbladder due to a stone.

    ① K80.00

    ② K80.01

    ③ K80.11

    ④ K80.00, K82.0

92. Female diagnosed with candidiasis endocarditis.

    ① B37.6

    ② B37.9

    ③ I39, B37.6

    ④ I39, B37.9

93. A 59-year-old male patient worked with talc for many years and is now diagnosed with pneumoconiosis.

    ① J60

    ② J62.0

    ③ J62.8

    ④ J63.6

94. A 17-year-old male has second-degree burns of both ankles and feet caused by fireworks.

    ① T24.121A, T24.122A, W39.xxxA

    ② T24.291A, T24.292S, W39.xxxD

    ③ T25.291A, T25.292A, W39.xxxA

    ④ T25.691A, T25.692A, W40.0xxA

95. The physician diagnosed the patient experiencing leakage of the mitral valve prosthesis.

    ① T82.01xA

    ② T82.03xA

    ③ T82.09xA

    ④ T82.223A

96. Patient is seen for carcinoma of the lower third of the esophagus.

    ① C15.3

    ② C15.4

    ③ C15.5

    ④ D13.0

97. Patient seen immediately after suffering a cut on the bottom of the left foot with an embedded sliver of wood.

    ① S91.311A

    ② S91.312A

    ③ S91.321A

    ④ S91.322A

98. The patient seen for anaphylactic shock as a result of eating shrimp.

    ① T78.02xA

    ② T78.03xA

    ③ T78.1xxA

    ④ T78.2xxA

99. This 44-year-old female patient is seen for plastic repair of a keloid scar of the left hand, a result of a previous burn.

    ① L91.0, T23.002A

    ② L91.0, T23.002S

    ③ L91.8, T23.002A

    ④ L91.8, T23.002D

100. A 2-year-old child seen in the physician's office after he placed a pebble in his left ear and the mother was unable to retrieve the stone.

    ① H92.02

    ② T16.1xxA

    ③ T16.2xxA

    ④ T16.2xxD

Name _____

Answer Sheet for Exam Questions: ICD-10-CM

1. ① ② ③ ④   30. ① ② ③ ④   59. ① ② ③ ④   88. ① ② ③ ④
2. ① ② ③ ④   31. ① ② ③ ④   60. ① ② ③ ④   89. ① ② ③ ④
3. ① ② ③ ④   32. ① ② ③ ④   61. ① ② ③ ④   90. ① ② ③ ④
4. ① ② ③ ④   33. ① ② ③ ④   62. ① ② ③ ④   91. ① ② ③ ④
5. ① ② ③ ④   34. ① ② ③ ④   63. ① ② ③ ④   92. ① ② ③ ④
6. ① ② ③ ④   35. ① ② ③ ④   64. ① ② ③ ④   93. ① ② ③ ④
7. ① ② ③ ④   36. ① ② ③ ④   65. ① ② ③ ④   94. ① ② ③ ④
8. ① ② ③ ④   37. ① ② ③ ④   66. ① ② ③ ④   95. ① ② ③ ④
9. ① ② ③ ④   38. ① ② ③ ④   67. ① ② ③ ④   96. ① ② ③ ④
10. ① ② ③ ④   39. ① ② ③ ④   68. ① ② ③ ④   97. ① ② ③ ④
11. ① ② ③ ④   40. ① ② ③ ④   69. ① ② ③ ④   98. ① ② ③ ④
12. ① ② ③ ④   41. ① ② ③ ④   70. ① ② ③ ④   99. ① ② ③ ④
13. ① ② ③ ④   42. ① ② ③ ④   71. ① ② ③ ④   100. ① ② ③ ④
14. ① ② ③ ④   43. ① ② ③ ④   72. ① ② ③ ④
15. ① ② ③ ④   44. ① ② ③ ④   73. ① ② ③ ④
16. ① ② ③ ④   45. ① ② ③ ④   74. ① ② ③ ④
17. ① ② ③ ④   46. ① ② ③ ④   75. ① ② ③ ④
18. ① ② ③ ④   47. ① ② ③ ④   76. ① ② ③ ④
19. ① ② ③ ④   48. ① ② ③ ④   77. ① ② ③ ④
20. ① ② ③ ④   49. ① ② ③ ④   78. ① ② ③ ④
21. ① ② ③ ④   50. ① ② ③ ④   79. ① ② ③ ④
22. ① ② ③ ④   51. ① ② ③ ④   80. ① ② ③ ④
23. ① ② ③ ④   52. ① ② ③ ④   81. ① ② ③ ④
24. ① ② ③ ④   53. ① ② ③ ④   82. ① ② ③ ④
25. ① ② ③ ④   54. ① ② ③ ④   83. ① ② ③ ④
26. ① ② ③ ④   55. ① ② ③ ④   84. ① ② ③ ④
27. ① ② ③ ④   56. ① ② ③ ④   85. ① ② ③ ④
28. ① ② ③ ④   57. ① ② ③ ④   86. ① ② ③ ④
29. ① ② ③ ④   58. ① ② ③ ④   87. ① ② ③ ④

Appendix—Selected Answers

Note that answers to the odd-numbered questions have been provided for you in this appendix to aid in your self-study. The remaining answers to the even-numbered questions are provided for instructors in our Instructor's Manual posted online (see Preface of this workbook for further details on the Instructor's Manual).

Worksheet Answers: 2015 CPT Codes

Evaluation and Management—I
2015 CPT Codes 99201–99239
1. 99217
3. 99205-25
5. 99213
7. 99281
9. 99212
11. 99214
13. 99235

Evaluation and Management—II
2015 CPT Codes 99241–99340
1. 99243
3. 99253-57
5. 99318
7. 99255
9. 99325
11. 99245
13. 99254
15. 99339

Evaluation and Management—III
2015 CPT Codes 99341–99499
1. 99347
3. 99477
5. 99367
7. 99461
9. 99386
11. 99360 q = 2
13. 99393
15. 99344

Anesthesia Services 2015 CPT
Codes 00100–01999
1. 01935
3. 01960
5. 01486-P3
7. 00214 and 99100
9. 00160
11. 00635
13. 01925
15. 01622

Integumentary System 2015 CPT
Codes 10021–19499
1. 15776
3. 11976
5. 13160
7. 11750-TA
9. 11100
11. 17110
13. 19000-RT
15. 12002
17. 11450-RT
19. 11622
21. 16030
23. 11010-LT
25. 15835-RT

Musculoskeletal System—I 2015
CPT Codes 20005–23929
1. 20206-RT
3. 20950-RT
5. 21116-LT
7. 23335-RT
9. 21049
11. 20694
13. 23800-RT
15. 23472-RT
17. 22222 and 22226 q = 1
19. 23044-LT
21. 20973-TA
23. 20101
25. 22830

Musculoskeletal System—II
2015 CPT Codes 23930–27299
1. 26045-LT
3. 26665-FA
5. 24100-RT
7. 25240-LT
9. 24685-LT
11. 25400-LT
13. 26560-RT
15. 25931-F1
17. 24566-LT
19. 26236-F3
21. 25449-LT
23. 26554-LT
25. 24342-LT

Musculoskeletal System—III
2015 CPT Codes 27301–29999
1. 29825-RT
3. 27331-LT
5. 29874-LT
7. 27524-LT
9. 28264-RT
11. 27603-LT
13. 27507-LT
15. 27695-RT
17. 27685-LT
19. 27422-RT
21. 27882-LT
23. 28530-LT
25. 28755-T5

Respiratory System 2015 CPT
Codes 30000–32999
1. 30130-LT
3. 31255
5. 31641
7. 31400
9. 32604
11. 31825
13. 31615
15. 31237
17. 30300
19. 31368
21. 30110
23. 31291
25. 32405-LT

Cardiovascular System 2015
CPT Codes 33010–37799
1. 37718-LT
3. 33534 and 33517
5. 33222
7. 33736
9. 36000-LT
11. 33915
13. 33945
15. 36600
17. 35636
19. 35112
21. 33011
23. 33476
25. 33681

Hemic and Lymphatic Systems 2015 CPT Codes 38100–39599

1. 38505
3. 39540
5. 38300-LT
7. 38525-RT
9. 38308
11. 38101
13. 38564
15. 38221
17. 39545
19. 38240
21. 39220
23. 38555-LT
25. 38571

Digestive System 2015 CPT Codes 40490–49999

1. 42700
3. 43846
5. 44147
7. 49505
9. 46221
11. 44391
13. 43771
15. 45388
17. 45910
19. 43425
21. 47120
23. 47802
25. 42950

Urinary System 2015 CPT Codes 50010–53899

1. 52441
3. 50500
5. 52234
7. 50815-RT
9. 51784
11. 52283
13. 50045
15. 53250
17. 50610
19. 52318
21. 51725
23. 50393
25. 52648

Male Genital System, Including Intersex Surgery 2015 CPT Codes 54000–55980

1. 54150-52
3. 55700
5. 55840
7. 55870
9. 55250
11. 55110
13. 55860

15. 54535
17. 55650-RT
19. 54560-50
21. 54865
23. 54420
25. 55970

Female Genital/Maternity 2015 CPT Codes 56405–59899

1. 58545
3. 58974
5. 57460
7. 59821
9. 59015
11. 58340
13. 59409 and 59412
15. 57545
17. 57720
19. 58240
21. 59515
23. 57288
25. 58559

Endocrine and Nervous Systems 2015 CPT Codes 60000–64999

1. 60254
3. 64760
5. 64893-LT
7. 63081
9. 61791
11. 64435
13. 61606
15. 61526
17. 61250-50
19. 63040
21. 60605
23. 64898-LT and 64902-RT
25. 62141

Eye and Ocular Adnexa 2015 CPT Codes 65091–68899

1. 68811-LT
3. 67413-LT
5. 65150-RT
7. 65260-LT
9. 66625-LT
11. 67904-RT
13. 67112-LT
15. 65286-RT
17. 68530-RT
19. 66820-LT
21. 66984-LT
23. 68761-RT
25. 67318-LT

Auditory System 2015 CPT Codes 69000–69990

1. 69710-LT
3. 69740 and 69990

5. 69145-RT
7. 69440-LT
9. 69820-LT
11. 69400-LT
13. 69745-LT
15. 69110-RT
17. 69540-LT
19. 69000-LT
21. 69910-LT
23. 69642-RT
25. 69220-RT

Radiology—I 2015 CPT Codes 70010–73725

1. 73580-26-LT
3. 73564-RT
5. 70492
7. 70030-LT
9. 71010
11. 70554
13. 72141
15. 72040-26
17. 71110
19. 73510-LT
21. 73010-LT
23. 71550
25. 72240-26

Radiology—II 2015 CPT Codes 74000–76499

1. 74241
3. 74230
5. 76120-26
7. 74455-26
9. 75966-26
11. 74270
13. 75658-26
15. 75887-26
17. 75791-26
17. 75605-26
19. 75801-26-RT
21. 74320-26
23. 75563-26

Radiology—III 2015 CPT Codes 76506–79999

1. 76805 and 76810 q = 1
3. 77285-RT
5. 78195
7. 77407
9. 76872
11. 78272
13. 76516
15. 78135
17. 77316
19. 79440
21. 78805
23. 76828
25. 78205

Pathology and Laboratory—I
2015 CPT Codes 80047–83885
1. 80426
3. 82270
5. 82131 q = 3
7. 80320
9. 82190
11. 81000
13. 82575
15. 83045
17. 80101 q = 1
19. 81025
21. 80074
23. 80412
25. 80439

Pathology and Laboratory—II
2015 CPT Codes 83915–86849
1. 84181
3. 84030
5. 84446
7. 86694
9. 85240
11. 86140
13. 85525
15. 84525
17. 84703
19. 84403
21. 84133
23. 84620
25. 86225

Pathology and Laboratory—III
2015 CPT Codes 86850–89356
1. 86965
3. 88348
5. 88045
7. 88182
9. 87804
11. 88304
13. 89320
15. 87184 q = 10
17. 88267
19. 88125
21. 86927 q = 2
23. 87806
25. 88331 and 88332 q = 1

Medicine—I 2015 CPT Codes
90281–92700
1. 92286
3. 90385
5. 92512
7. 91122
9. 92081-RT
11. 90471 and 90747
13. 90959

15. 90846
17. 92235
19. 92567
21. 92552
23. 90870
25. 90837

Medicine—II 2015 CPT Codes
92920–96020
1. 92977
3. 93660-26
5. 95868
7. 93888
9. 95827
11. 95004 q = 10, and 95017 q = 3
13. 93225
15. 95970
17. 93600
19. 93965
21. 94760
23. 93351
25. 95933

Medicine—III 2015 CPT Codes
96040–0339T
1. 99507
3. 97033 q = 2
5. 98925
7. 98968
9. 3288F
11. 96902
13. 96154 q = 2
15. 99502
17. 97002
19. 99511
21. 96422
23. 96401
25. 99601

Worksheet Answers: 2015 HCPCS Level II Codes

HCPCS Level II Codes 2015 HCPCS
1. V5060
3. J0558
5. M0300
7. L3360-RT
9. J0780
11. A4358 q = 1
13. Q0091
15. A0130-PR
17. E0105

19. J9280
21. L6635
23. A4210 q = 1
25. E0619

Modifiers 2015 CPT
1. 24
3. 32
5. 57

Modifiers 2015 HCPCS
1. AH
3. QD
5. AR

Worksheet Answers: 2015 ICD-10/9-CM Codes

Answers to Medical Necessity Exercise
1. D
3. D
5. C

1—Infectious/ParasiticDiseases 2015 ICD-10/9-CM
1.	A06	006
3.	A17	137
5.	B85	132
7.	B65	120
9.	B80	127
1.	B30.1	077.0
3.	A27.89	100.89
5.	B35.9	110.9
7.	A50.57	090.5
9.	A90	061
11.	A03.0	004.0
13.	A54.02	098.0
15.	A01.3	002.3
17.	N39.0 + B96.20	599.0 + 041.49
19.	A41.4	038.3
21.	A30.9	030.2
23.	A98.4	078.89
25.	A87.1	049.1

2—Neoplasms 2015 ICD-10/9-CM
1.	C02	141
3.	D04	232

5. C25	157		
7. D05	233		
9. C34	162		

1. C34.31	162.5
3. C00.1	140.1
5. C79.31	198.3
7. C71.4	191.4
9. D30.4	223.81
11. C78.6	197.6
13. D30.11	223.1
15. C48.1	158.8
17. C49.3	171.4
19. D02.1	231.1
21. C85.94	202.84
23. C34.32 + Z72.0	165.5
25. C09.1	146.2

3—Blood and Blood-Forming 2015 ICD-10/9-CM

1. D67	286
3. D64	285
5. D51	281
7. D72	288
9. D75	289

1. D68.318	286.59
3. D69.59	287.49
5. D53.1	281.3
7. D57.1	282.61
9. D61.810	284.11
11. D59.4	283.19
13. D68.0	286.4
15. D66	286.0
17. D73.89	289.59
19. D72.1	288.3
21. D56.8	282.49
23. D72.810	288.51
25. D52.0	281.2

4—Endocrine/Metabolic Disease 2015 ICD-10/9-CM

1. E10	250
3. E04	241
5. E88	277
7. E13	249
9. E31	258

1. E06.3	245.2
3. E10.36	250.51 + 366.41
5. E50.5	264.5
7. E11.610	250.61 + 713.5
9. E78.1	272.1
11. E78.2	272.2
13. E73.9	271.3
15. E42	260
17. E10.621 + L97.421	250.81 + 707.14
19. E30.0	259.0

21. E71.521	277.86
23. E84.0	277.02
25. E36.02	998.11 + 998.12

5—Mental and Behavioral Disorders 2015 ICD-10/9-CM

1. F98	307
3. F34	300
5. F22	297
7. F07	310
9. F10	291

1. F11.20	304.00
3. F60.5	301.4
5. F84.5	299.80
7. F53	648.44
9. F10.229	303.00
11. F65.2	302.4
13. F40.231	300.29
15. F16.122	305.30
17. F90.2	314.01
19. F40.10	300.09
21. F43.23	309.28
23. F44.81	300.14
25. F94.1	313.89

6—Nervous System 2015 ICD-10/9-CM

1. G00	320
3. G12	335
5. G96	349
7. G56	354
9. G20	332

1. G57.51	355.5
3. G97.0	997.09
5. G31.83	313.82
7. G47.411	347.01
9. G00.9	320.9
11. G62.81	357.82
13. G83.4	344.61
15. G30.0	331.0
17. T51.1x1S + G72.2	359.4 + E860.2
19. G61.81	357.81
21. G03.1	322.2
23. G12.0	335.0
25. G44.229	339.12

7—Eye and Adnexa 2015 ICD-10/9-CM

1. H02	374
3. H16	370
5. H25	366
7. H33	361
9. H52	367

1. H52.213	367.22
3. H35.123	362.23
5. H01.134	373.31

7. H40.122	365.12 + 365.72
9. H21.242	364.54
11. H02.812 + Z18.10	374.86 + V90.10
13. H31.023	363.31
15. H40.1221	365.12 + 365.71
17. H16.133	370.24
19. H44.711 + Z18.10	360.61 + V90.10
21. H34.811	362.35
23. H55.04	379.55
25. H59.812	997.99 + 363.30

8—Ear and Mastoid 2015 ICD-10/9-CM

1. H71	385
3. H81	386
5. H73	384
7. H91	388
9. H90	389

1. H92.01	388.70
3. H91.22	388.2
5. H83.11	386.40
7. H72.2x2	384.23
9. H81.42	386.2
11. H68.111	381.61
13. H95.02	383.32
15. H83.3x3	388.12
17. H61.23	380.4
19. H83.02	386.30
21. H71.21	385.33
23. H74.41	385.32
25. H65.23 + Z77.22	381.10

9—Circulatory System 2015 ICD-10/9-CM

1. I95	458
3. I50	428
5. I05	394
7. I83	454
9. I33	421

1. I08.0	396.2
3. I11.9	402.90
5. I20.0	411.1
7. I63.012	433.21
9. I25.2	412
11. I71.4	441.4
13. I97.2	457.0
15. I80.12	451.11
17. I42.6 + F10.20	425.5 + 303.90
19. I73.9	443.9
21. I21.02	410.11
23. I73.00	443.0
25. I48.2	427.31

10—Respiratory System 2015 ICD-10/9-CM

1. J81	514
3. J00	465
5. J68	506
7. J36	475
9. J20	466

1. J30.1	477.0
3. J35.01	474.00
5. J38.4	478.6
7. J09.x1	488.81
9. J84.112	516.31
11. J42	491.9
13. J96.11	518.83
15. J93.83	512.89
17. J70.5	508.2
19. J69.0	507.0
21. J04.2	464.20
23. J15.212	482.42
25. J43.9	492.8

11—Digestive System 2015 ICD-10/9-CM

1. K40	550
3. K74	571
5. K95	539
7. K50	550
9. K81	575

1. K11.8	527.8
3. K58.9	564.1
5. K01.1	520.6
7. K43.6	553.20
9. K61.0	566
11. K12.0	528.2
13. K91.1	564.2
15. B65.9 + K77	573.8
17. K80.45	574.41
19. K26.7	532.70
21. K63.5	211.3
23. K05.10	523.10
25. T51.1x2S + K52.1	558.2 + 909.1 + E950.9

12—Skin/Subcutaneous Tissue 2015 ICD-10/9-CM

1. L13	694
3. L02	680
5. L74	705
7. L21	690
9. L05	685

1. L93.0	695.4
3. L76.11	998.2
5. L01.03	684
7. L50.8	708.8
9. L29.0	698.0
11. L70.0	706.1
13. L89.212	707.04 + 707.22
15. L02.32	680.5
17. L24.81	692.83
19. L57.8	692.70
21. L72.3	706.2
23. L63.1	704.09
25. I87.311 + L97.213	459.31 + 707.12

13—Musculo/Connective 2015 ICD-10/9-CM

1. M10	274
3. M71	719
5. M25	719
7. M77	726
9. M85	733
1. M67.01	727.81
3. M24.462	718.36
5. M54.5	724.2
7. M27.3	526.5
9. M67.432	727.41
11. M32.9	710.0
13. M02.022	713.1
15. M75.112	726.13
17. M21.41 + M21.42	734
19. M70.51	726.60
21. M48.52xD	733.13
23. M62.831	728.85
25. M80.051A	733.14

14—Genitourinary System 2015 ICD-10/9-CM

1. N32	596
3. N60	610
5. N05	582
7. N75	616
9. N47	605

1. N18.2	585.2
3. N70.13	614.1
5. N63	611.72
7. N99.512	596.82
9. N39.3	788.32
11. N80.0	617.0
13. N99.3	618.5
15. N00.9	580.9
17. N13.30	591
19. N91.0	626.0
21. N48.30	607.3
23. N98.1	256.1 + 997.89
25. N46.9	606.9

15—Pregnancy/Childbirth 2015 ICD-10/9-CM

1. O00	633
3. O83	634
5. O23	646
7. O22	671
9. O9A	995

1. O71.1	665.10
3. O26.03, Z3A.29	646.10
5. O01.1	630
7. O09.291	V23.5
9. O03.82	634.30
11. O92.13	676.14
13. O60.23x0, Z37.0, Z3A.30	644.21 + V27.0
15. O00.9 + O08.4	633.90 + 639.3
17. O04.82	635.30
19. O62.3	661.30
21. O69.82x0	663.31
23. O87.2	671.82
25. O02.1, Z3A.16	632

16—Perinatal Period 2015 ICD-10/9-CM

1. P04	760
3. P22	770
5. P10	767
7. P59	774
9. P08	766

1. P01.6	761.6
3. P05.18	764.08
5. P35.0	771.0
7. P23.4	770.0 + 041.4
9. P36.2	771.81 + 041.19
11. P08.21	766.21
13. P58.0	774.1
15. P92.1	779.33
17. P93.0	779.4
19. P25.1	770.2
21. P96.1	779.5
23. P27.0	770.7
25. P84	770.88

17—Congenital Abnormalities 2015 ICD-10/9-CM

1. Q16	744
3. Q03	742
5. Q38	750
7. Q36	749
9. Q82	757

1. Q99.2	759.83
3. Q54.1	752.61
5. Q70.33	755.13
7. Q33.0	748.4
9. Q75.0	756.0
11. Q05.7	741.93
13. Q07.01	741.00
15. Q76.0	756.17

17.	Q78.0	756.51	3.	S82.822K	733.82	
19.	Q40.2	750.7	5.	T15.02xA	930.0 + E914	
21.	Q45.0	751.7	7.	T82.01xA	996.02	
23.	Q61.5	753.17	9.	T74.11xA	995.81	
25.	Q79.4	756.71	11.	S02.64xD	802.24	

17. V94.22xA   Y92.828 +
                Y93.16
19. W21.09xA   Y92.318 +
                Y93.73
21. V85.5xxA
23. W89.1xxA
25. X08.11xA   Y92.59

18—Signs/Symptoms 2015 ICD-10/9-CM

13. S33.140D   839.20
15. T39.012A   965.1 + E950.0
17. S08.121A   872.01
19. T63.041S   909.1 + E929.1
21. T78.40xD   995.3
23. S97.111A   928.3
25. T28.1xxA + 947.2 +
    X10.0xxA   E924.0

1. R00   427
3. R06   786
5. R11   787
7. R41   780
9. R59   785

1. A41.2 +   038.10 + 995.92
   R65.21   + 785.52
3. R42   780.4
5. R87.619   795.00
7. R18.8   568.82
9. R41.83   V62.89
11. R14.3   787.3
13. R25.3   781.0
15. R23.2   782.62
17. R54   797
19. R09.2   799.1
21. R23.4   782.8
23. R40.3   780.03
25. R30.9   788.1

20—Causes of Morbidity 2015 ICD-10/9-CM

1. V00   E003
3. W45   E920
5. Y65   E878
7. W61   E906
9. V97   E841

1. V01.09xA   Y92.830 +
              Y93.F9
3. X36.1xxA
5. W31.2xxA   Y92.015 +
              Y93.H3
7. Y07.421
9. V73.6xxA   Y92.410
11. W56.21xA Y92.832 +
              Y93.18
13. Y95.01xA
15. W16.621A Y92.828 +
              Y93.11

21—Factors Influencing Health 2015 ICD-10/9-CM

1. Z02   V70
3. Z81   V61
5. Z79   V58
7. Z86   V12
9. Z60

1. Z01.419   V72.31
3. Z56.4   V62.1
5. Z74.3   V60.89
7. Z73.1   V69.8
9. Z98.84   V45.86
11. Z86.12   V12.02
13. Z13.1   V77.1
15. S52.352D V57.1
17. Z76.0   V68.1
19. Z46.51   V53.51
21. Z16.11   V09.0
23. Z90.710 V88.01
25. Z91.013 V15.04

19—Poisoning/External Causes 2015 ICD-10/9-CM

1. N63 +   611.72 +
   S20.161S   906.2

Instructions for Submitting an Exam to Cengage for CEU Approval

The American Academy of Professional Coders (AAPC) is granting approval for CEU credits to qualified candidates for the successful completion of the 30-question exam associated with the *2015 Coding Workbook for the Physician's Office*, ISBN 978-1-3052-5913-3, by Alice Covell. The AAPC will grant prior approval for a total of one and a half (1.5) CEU credits for completion of this exam with a passing grade of 70% or better. To apply for CEU credit on this title, you will need to print out the exam posted to the Premium Website for the 2015 workbook and return the completed exam to Cengage Learning, for grading. For further instructions, access the Premium Website by going to www.cengagebrain.com. In the search field in the upper right corner of the screen, type "Covell." A pop-up screen will appear asking for login information; simply click "I Don't Have an Access Code or Course Key" and search for the *2015 Coding Workbook for the Physician's Office* and you will be able to access the free AAPC-related materials posted.

Please note: Awarding of a CEU certificate from Cengage Learning does not constitute full CEU approval. You will be responsible for submitting the awarded certificate to the AAPC the next time your credential is up for renewal in order to officially obtain the CEU credit(s).

This program has the prior approval of the American Academy of Professional Coders (AAPC) for 1.5 continuing education hours. Grant of prior approval in no way constitutes endorsement by the AAPC of the program content or program sponsor. For more information on obtaining CEUs, please go to www.aapc.com

181